BRIDPO

&

LYME REGIS

The Story of
Dorset's Western Coast

Rodney Legg

Dorset Publishing Company
National School North Street Wincanton Somerset BA9 9AT

For my mentor **John Fowles**
from the "Satan of Sherborne"
as he once described his
tempting purveyor of Lyme's
scarcest old books

Publishing details
First published 1999. Copyright Rodney Legg © 1999.
Published by Dorset Publishing Company at the Wincanton Press, National School, North Street, Wincanton, Somerset BA9 9AT (01-963-32583) to whom updatings may be sent, addressed to the author. Distributed by Halsgrove, Lower Moor Way, Tiverton, Devon EX16 6SS (01-884-243-242).

Printing credits
Typeset in $12^1/_2$ on 15pt Forlane by Julie Green. Illustrated by the author from his photographs and collection. Printed in Somerset by F. W. B. Printing at Bennetts Mead, Southgate Road, Wincanton BA9 9EB (01-963-33755).

International standard book number
ISBN 0-948699-66-3

Old Bridport

Shingle gathering: from the beach below East Cliff at West Bay.

Turner print: West Bay and a lively sea, from J. M. W. Turner's coastal plates published in 1849.

West Bay: showing how the channel into Bridport Harbour was created between two solid piers.

Historic look: apart from the building of Pier Terrace, West Bay would look much the same into the mid-20th century.

The basin: Bridport Harbour at West Bay, looking across to the quay and Pier Terrace.

Rough sea: a southerly gale renders the ship channel inoperable at West Bay.

Jaws motif: on a boat beached at low tide in the basin at West Bay.

Sea fishing: from the end of West Pier, beside the harbour channel at West Bay.

Harbour Museum: in the old Salt House at West Bay, with cannon retrieved from shipwrecks.

Bridport Arms: among the front row in the cluster of thatch looking seawards from West Bay.

Free food: gulls in the backwater and River Brit, across from the George Hotel.

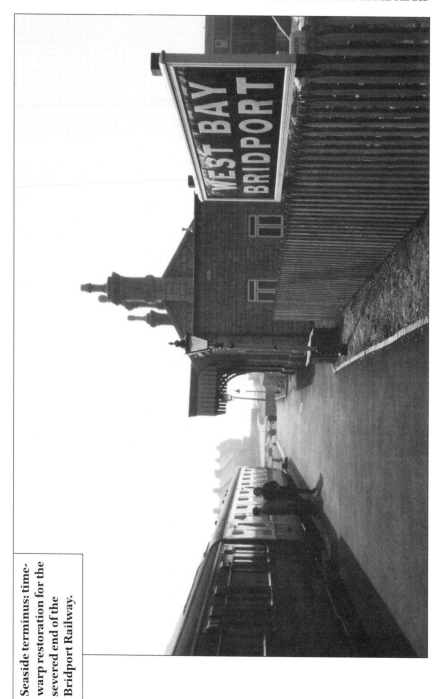

Seaside terminus: time-warp restoration for the severed end of the Bridport Railway.

Bridport Station: seen in its heyday, with double platforms, in 1906.

Single line: twilight moment, with the driver having to do the gates, when Dr Beeching's axe had struck at the Bridport Railway.

Bridport town: sheltered in the folds a mile inland from West Bay, amid fields just asking for a bypass to be built.

Ancient church: St Mary's in Bridport has a 13th-century plan and a 15th-century tower, but was lengthened at each end in 1860.

Mediaeval knight: in chain mail armour, with shield and broken sword, this 13th-century effigy being in St Mary's church.

East Street: looking towards the Town Hall in the centre of Bridport.

Georgian brick: the sunny side of the Town Hall at Bridport, seen from South Street.

Bull Hotel: scene of a shoot-out during the Monmouth Rebellion, in East Street, Bridport.

Arts Centre: 1838-built in the centre of Bridport, as a Wesleyan Methodist Chapel.

The Chantry: Bridport's mediaeval house, in South Street.

Bridport Museum: housed in an old building in South Street that used to be known as 'The Castle'.

Portland stone: classical Georgian lines of the Literary and Scientific Institute at Bridport.

Timber framed: 17th-century house, since refronted in rendered brick, next to the Book Shop (coned-off for road works) in South Street, Bridport.

Two inns: The Volunteer and The Woodman, with hardly a tree between them, in South Street at Bridport.

Quaker rooms: the Society of Friends' 17th-century meeting house in South Street, Bridport.

Taylor's Charity: the almshouse in South Street, Bridport, was founded by Quaker Daniel Taylor.

Barrack Street: formerly Stake Lane, at Bridport.

Bridport Hospital: the present big building of Barracks Street, where the garrison headquarters of Napoleonic times became a Public Assistance Institution.

Palmer's Brewery: poster for Britain's only thatched brewery (centre, foreground) dating from 1794 when it was founded by S. Gundry and Company.

Water-wheel: inscribed for maker T. Helyear, 1879, beside Bridport Brewery, operated a pump rather than taking water from the River Brit.

East Bridge: 1784-dated, with 18th-century houses overlooking the River Brit at Bridport.

Bridport floods: East Road, with the approaching vehicle coming over the railway level crossing, on 28 November 1929.

Happy Island: the closest Edwardian picnic spot within reach of Bridport town.

East Pier: protecting the channel into the basin of Bridport Harbour at West Bay, with East Cliff beyond.

Coastal Chronicles

774   King Cynewulf has granted land on the west bank of the River Lim to the Abbot of Sherborne. [Being the Sherborne Lane area of Lyme, where salt-panning was carried out.]

1145   A Papal Bull, signed in Rome by Pope Eugenius III, confirms the granting of Lyme and its fishing to the Abbey of Sherborne.

1157   In the five years since the marriage of Eleanor of Aquitaine [divorcee of King Louis VII of France] to Henry of Anjou [King Henry II of England] and the ceding to England of the part of Aquitaine to which she is heiress, the merchants of Lyme have found new wealth. Outgoing cargoes of West Country wool are exchanged at Bordeaux for the fine wines of the Garonne Valley.

1261   Gilbert of London, acting on a commission from King Henry III, has required the Bailiffs of Lyme to provide vessels to carry Queen Eleanor and Prince Edward to France.

1284   The royal cachet, Regis, has been bestowed on the Dorset town of Lyme by King Edward [the First].

1295   Two burgesses of the free borough of Lyme Regis have been summoned by the King to attend the calling of a Parliament.

1320   The tongue of land at Lyme that runs into the sea [from Cobb Gate], on which stood the warehouses and quay, has been washed away in a great storm. Seventy dwellings have been lost.

circa 1340   A Leper Asylum and Infirmary, dedicated to St Mary and the Holy Spirit, has been established beside a spring on a stream-side terrace above the River Lim in Lyme Regis. [Its site is now the Lepers Well garden, between Coombe Street and the

Angel Inn. Only two such wells have survived in England, with the other being in Winchester and dedicated to St Mary Magdalene. The dreaded disease's most famous victim, in 1329, was Robert the Bruce, the King and liberator of Scotland from the English.]

1342 Two "better and discreter mariners" of Lyme are summoned to a Parliament at Westminster to advice on ways to improve the production of ships for the wars in Scotland and France.

1347 Lyme has supplied four ships and 62 seamen for the siege of Paris.

1349 Fear of the Black Death, spreading as a plague across Europe, has caused the order to be sent to Lyme and other ports that no one is to be embarked at its harbour, other than merchants or well-known messengers.

1385 A haven is being constructed at the estuary of the River Brit, to the south of Bridport, by John Huddersfield. He does not have the means to complete the work and has asked for Crown approval to levy tolls on boats using the new waterway.

1401 Collections have been made in Bridport to raise sufficient money for the clearance of the blocked and damaged waterway at the mouth of the River Brit.

1414 Rocks and piles in the estuary of the River Brit at Bridport are a danger to navigation and the townspeople are subscribing towards the rebuilding of their haven.

1481 The Burgesses of Lyme have petitioned the King that their town is often wasted by the tides and the overflowing of the sea, causing many inhabitants to depart, and that the port [the first Cobb, named for its sea-pebble walling] "was by tempest destroyed". In response the King [Edward IV] has granted the town freedom from "fee-farm" taxation for a period of 65 years.

1558   The estuaries at Bridport Haven and nearby Charmouth are no longer regarded as navigable and will in future be treated as creeks, under the jurisdiction of Lyme Regis.

1569   Johanna Ellesdon, a widow of Lyme Regis, has upon her oath declared that Ellen Walker is a witch, who was seen to vomit pins and needles.

1570   Lyme's townspeople frequently discuss ways of protecting their wealth from outrages by man – with ordnance, powder and shot – and from nature; with great piles to withstand the violence and fretting of the sea. They also feel the need to be protected from the intemperate behaviour of one another. A bylaw has been passed by the borough requiring discussions to be conducted without vehemence or indecent words, on penalty of a 40 shilling fine to be paid on the Cobb.

1586   In anticipation of a gathering Spanish Armada, coastal features around Lyme Regis have been surveyed and the plan placed in Queen Elizabeth's library, in case of an attempt being made by the enemy to land at the Cobb. Sixty troops have been posted there to repel landing parties. The port is to fit out two ships, the 60-ton *Revenge* and 90-ton *Jacob*, as its contribution to the English Fleet.

1588 – Sunday 21 July.   Don Miguele de Oquendo's flagship *San Salvador*, carrying the paymaster and treasure chests of the Spanish Armada, lost much of her stern and superstructure in an explosion off the Devon coast. She was partially emptied by the enemy and then abandoned, to drift across Lyme Bay with injured crew still on board, and is now off the Chesil Beach. Captain

Flemyng, in the pinnace *Golden Hind*, will secure her with a line and tow her around Portland Bill into Portland Roads, the anchorage off Weymouth.

1589   Lyme Regis, it appears from Bree's maritime survey, is the third largest port in England, behind London and Bristol. London itself has six times the number of ships.

1590   The barque *Cherubim* has founded trading posts at Senegal and the Gambia on the coast of West Africa, from which elephants' tusks and gold-dust are the new commodities being shipped back to Lyme. [Customs dues at Lyme would reach the then colossal total of £5,000 per year; two per cent of the national take.]

1591   Sir Richard Grenville in the Lyme vessel *Revenge*, operating with the Azores Fleet of Lord Thomas Howard in the interception of Spanish treasure ships, found himself isolated from the remainder of the English vessels, off Flores. The *Revenge* fought alone against **15** Spanish ships but Sir Richard refused to surrender. He died of his wounds; though many of the crew survived.

1591   Queen Elizabeth has confirmed the royal charter of the "ancient and populous borough" of Lyme Regis "which may for ever remain a town of peace and quietness to the fear and terror of evil men."

1603   Sir George Somers, the retired buccaneer and veteran of three voyages to the Azores, was knighted by King James [the First] at Whitehall on 23 July. He has returned to his west Dorset home, Berne Farm at Whitchurch Canonicorum in the coastal hinterland of Charmouth, which he bought in 1587.

1604 – 25 February.   Sir George Somers, the retired seafarer, has been elected Member of Parliament for Lyme Regis.

circa 1605 The death has taken place at Lyme Regis of Arthur Gregory, who distinguished himself in the Elizabethan age as one of the first great names in the annals of the secret intelligence service. International conspiracies are carried out through correspondence and Gregory had the admirable art of forcing the seal of a letter, yet so invisible that it still appeared a virgin impression to even the most exact beholder. Secretary Walsingham made great use of him, about the interception of the diplomatic packet which passed from foreign parts to Mary Queen of Scotland. He had a pension sent unto him, for his good service, out of the Exchequer.

1609 – 23 May.   King James has appointed Sir George Somers of Whitchurch Canonicorum as Admiral of the Association of the South Virginian Company. He is fitting out a fleet of nine ships to convey a fresh band of colonists across the Atlantic Ocean to Jamestown which is troubled by native unrest and a want of food and supplies.

1610 News has reached England that the expedition for the relief of the Virginia colony was scattered by a hurricane when it was eight weeks out in mid-Atlantic. The commander of the fleet, Sir George Somers in *Sea Venture*, was wrecked on the rocks of the islands known as the Bermudas from the Spaniard, Juan Bermudas, who first sighted them in 1515. There, on 25 July 1609, Sir George's crew found their salvation with abundant food in the form of easily caught shoals of fish, turtles, hogs, fowl, eggs, and edible fruit. There was also timber, which enabled them to build two ships, *Patience* and *Providence*, which enabled them to sail again for Virginia, on 10 May 1610. Meanwhile the possession of Bermudas, which are now to be known as Virginiola, has been established in the name of King James and Sir George has left a group of men there to ensure continuance of the British claim.

1610 – 23 May. The salvation of Jamestown and its distressed Virginian colonists, with the arrival of the vessels from Bermuda, to be followed shortly [in two weeks] by Thomas West and another relief party from England.

1610 The adventures of Sir George Somers and the *Sea Venture* which was wrecked on an uninhabited chain of islands in the mid-Atlantic has been recorded by another Lyme man, Silvester Jourdain, who was accompanying his townsman, as *A Discovery of the Bermudas, otherwise called the Isle of Devils*. [A copy found its way into the hands of playwright William Shakespeare who was inspired to begin work on *The Tempest*.]

1610 – 9 November. Sir George Somers [born 1554] dies in the Bermudas from what is described as "a surfeit of eating a pig". His heart has been buried here [St George, Bermuda], beneath a wooden cross, but the body is being embalmed for return to England [where it is buried, with military honours, in the parish church at Whitchurch Canonicorum].

1611 – 19 June. Matthew Somers, having returned to Britain with the body of his late uncle, Sir George Somers, has set sail back to the islands of the Bermudas with a supply of fish and hogs for onward transit to the hunger-stricken colonists of Jamestown, Virginia.

1644 – 11 February. King Charles, at his court in Oxford, has today signed the command to Sir John Stawell [1599-1662], Governor of Taunton, ordering forces to be sent against Lyme Regis: "Whereas we understand ye condition of ye rebellious town of Lyme to be such, as (by God's blessing) ye present addition of some few more foot forces may bring the same into our submission and obedience; we have therefore thought fit to require you forthwith to send 200 of your foot together with their arms and pay, to that work (the like whereof we have ordered Colonel Wyndham to do also) to be returned back again to you at the end of that service, which we conceive and hope will be speedily. And hereof we desire you by no means to fail. And this Our Letter shall be your Warrant on that behalf. Given at Our Court at Oxford ye 11th day of February 1643 [1644 actually; until the calendar change of 1751 the year's end was 31 March]. By his Majesty's Command. Edward Nicholas." [Sir Edward Nicholas, 1593-1669, Secretary of State to the King. The letter was acquired in 1981 by the present author, Rodney Legg, and donated by him to the town's Philpot Museum.]"

1644   Royalist forces led by Prince Maurice of the Rhine besieged the Cromwellian town of Lyme Regis for eight weeks, in a siege that was abandoned on 16 June 1644. They failed to take their primary objective, the Cobb harbour, which at this time is a detached quay separated by an area of foreshore from the adjacent mainland. The town's fleet of boats broke the land blockade and thatch was stripped from roofs to reduce the danger from flaming arrows that rained down on the town from the attackers on the hill. Exchanges of musket-fire from either side of the earthwork defences to the town amounted to little more than mutual harassment though an evening raid accounted for Lyme's most effective defender; Captain Pyne commanded its cavalry regiment and had for a year taken the Civil War into the Royalist camp with repeated sallies against their positions. The other heroes were the town's determined womenfolk who sustained the resistance and produced a minor epic of the conflict, in a set of verses that are establishing them as a legend for Puritan London. Rev James Strong, the rector of Bettiscombe, in the hills beyond Marshwood Vale, is the author of *Joanereidos*, which carries the following explanatory sub-title – "Feminine valour: eminently discovered in Western women: as well as by defying the merciless enemy at the face abroad, as by fighting against them in the Garrison towns, sometimes carrying stones, anon tumbling of stones over the Works on the enemy, when they have been scaling them, some carrying powder, others charging pieces to ease the soldiers, constantly resolved for generality, not to think any one's life dear, to maintain that Christian quarrel for the Parliament. Whereby, as they deserve commendations in themselves, so are they prepared as example unto others."

1651   Defeated at the Battle of Worcester, where he fled from the vicinity of St Martin's Gate, Worcester, on the evening of 3 September, vanquished monarch Charles II embarked on one of history's great escapes. It saw him disguised as a girl servant and hiding in an oak tree – spawning a forest of Royal Oak pub names – and secreted in priest holes, such as that in Trent Manor on the borders of Somerset and Dorset. From here he crossed west Dorset, via Broadwindsor, but had to abort his intended plan to find a boat at Charmouth, turning eastwards, almost being captured by troops at the [Old] George Inn in the centre of Bridport and escaping along Lee Lane at Bradpole [23 September 1651; commemorated by a rough-hewn block of Bothenhampton stone erected by Alexander Meyrick Broadley on the anniversary in 1901]. The last leg of the royal route would end at Shoreham, aboard the *Surprise*, which took him to exile in France.

1653 – 18 February.   People listen and watch from the cliffs at West Bay as what is nearly a disaster for both the English and Dutch fleets unfolds at the eastern end of Lyme Bay, off Portland. Admiral Robert Blake was lucky to escape with his life, and Maarten Harpertszoon Tromp was fortunate to survive with the bulk of his ships. Blake had blundered by taking his red squadron alone to intercept Tromp's full fleet. The English flagship *Triump* (sic) was heavily engaged, with the loss of the captain, and Blake was severely wounded. Not until the afternoon did Vice-Admiral Sir William Penn arrive with the blue and white squadrons of the English fleet to make an even battle. [By the next morning the ships were off St Catherine's Point, Isle of Wight, and Tromp escaped up-Channel. He had lost five warships sunk and four captured, and 40 merchant ships were also lost, but the main Dutch fleet survived to fight again.]

1653 – 20 June.   From a deep black cloud "it rained warm blood" on the Dorset coast today, supposedly from the sea where the British and Dutch fleets fought in the Channel, the blood having somehow been sucked into the sky. [Similar red rain fell in the Isle of Wight in 1176; the colour and the fact the rain in 1653 was warm suggest that the phenomenon is caused by Saharan dust being blown high into the sky, rather than the fallout of ash from a volcanic eruption.]

1662   Dr Thomas Fuller, rector of Broadwindsor, writing in his *History of the Worthies of England*, records a Dorsetshire proverb – "Stabbed with a Bridport dagger; that is, hanged, or executed at the gallows." His explanation is that, much, if not most hemp (for the quantity of ground) grows about Bridport, a market town in this county: "And hence it is, that there is an ancient Statute (though now disused and neglected) that the cable ropes for the Navy Royal were to be made thereabouts, as affording the best tackling for that purpose."

1684 – Christmas.   Five persons have died at Fleet, a coastal hamlet behind the Chesil Beach, from exposure after trying to leave Weymouth for home, towards Bridport, in "a tremendous storm" on 23 December.

1685 – 11 June.   This Thursday morning a Dutch vessel anchored in Lyme Bay and two men were rowed ashore at Seatown beach, in the parish of Chideock. An Englishman, Thomas Dare, was accompanied by Andrew, Lord Fletcher; a fiery Scot. The latter was the second-in-command of exiled Protestant Duke of Monmouth's rebel cavalry, preparing a Western Rebellion to challenge Catholic King James II for the Stuart crown. They are to make their way to liaise with landowning sympathisers at Forde Abbey, near Chard.

1685 – 11 June.   James Scott, Duke of Monmouth, landed in England this evening with 82 of his men – to claim the throne of England from his uncle, James II. They came ashore from the Dutch frigate *Helderenburg* on the pebble beach to the west of the Cobb harbour at Lyme Regis, and unfurled a green banner with gold embroidered lettering: "Fear nothing but God." The party set off up the Stile Path [as Cobb Road was then] to foment rebellion.

1685 – 13 June.   The Duke of Monmouth's advance party has bungled its task, after leaving Forde Abbey to join the main force at Lyme Regis. Andrew Fletcher pulled rank to seize a horse which Thomas Dare had commandeered. The Englishman refused and raised his whip, at which Fletcher raised his gun, and shot him through the head. Volunteers who witnessed the incident wanted Fletcher strung up for murder but he was smuggled back on ship. [He would escape to Spain. These disastrous double own-goals deprived Monmouth of two key players. Fletcher could have been invaluable – an aggressive Scot was just what Monmouth would lack at the head of his cavalry for a skirmish at Bridport and the final rout at the Battle of Sedgemoor in the Somerset Levels, on 5 July 1685. Thomas Dare also held a vital position, as the paymaster for the operation.]

1685 – 14 June.   The Bull Inn in East Street at Bridport, in which officers of the Dorset Militia based themselves, has been the scene of the first skirmish of the Duke of Monmouth's campaign. Colonel Thomas Venner led the Red Regiment of rebel cavalry through the town. Shots were fired at them from windows at the hostelry. Monmouth's men then broke down its doors but several lives were lost in the process, including those of Dorset gentlemen Edward Coker of Mappowder and Wadham Strangways of Abbotsbury, who were killed by Colonel Venner. Two of the King's men managed to escape, one into an attic, and the other hiding in a plot of kidney beans. A shot from the dark wounded Colonel Venner in the stomach, following which he gave the order to retreat and Lord Grey's supporting horsemen also bolted, westwards to Charmouth, at the sound of gunfire. Major Nathaniel Wade restored discipline and prepared to hold the bridge over the River Brit with his foot-soldiers but the Dorset Militia contented themselves with an arms-length exchange of insults.

1685 – 12 September. The following dozen persons, condemned by Lord Chief Justice Jeffreys for their part in the shambolic Western Rebellion, were today hanged, drawn and quartered beside the Monmouth Beach landing place of the unfortunate Duke. It is observed by Mr Pitts, who was a spectator, that they were to have been drawn to the place of execution by a sledge, but that no cart-horses, or even coach-horses, could be made to draw it, so that they were obliged to go on foot. This was much remarked at the time, and was considered by many as a kind of miracle. Each is to be fully disembowelled and butchered. Their body parts will be distributed for display across the affected counties as a gruesome warning of the price for treason.

1.   Lieutenant-Colonel Abraham Holmes, an old and gallant officer, who had served under Cromwell with distinguished reputation. He accompanied the Duke to Holland, by whom he was made a Major-General. In the action at Norton St Philip one of his arms was shot to pieces so that it hung only by the flesh; and in consequence of this being soon taken, was stripped by the soldiers and carried naked before a Justice of the Peace who humanely clothed him. His shattered arm being an encumbrance to him, he laid it on a dresser and cut it off himself with the cook-maid's knife. He was hanged on the very spot where he landed with the Duke.

2.   Christopher Battiscombe was a young gentleman, who lived near Lyme. He was several times at the Judge's lodgings, who offered him pardon if he would impeach others, which he nobly refused. Among the petitioners for his life was a young lady to whom he was engaged to be married; who making her humble request on her knees to the Judge, his insulting cruelty dictated

this reply: That he could only spare her part of him; but as he knew what she wanted, it should be that part which she liked best, and he would give orders to the sheriff accordingly.

3.   Lieutenant William Hewling, but 20-years-old, whose brother Benjamin suffered similarly at Taunton. They were fashionable Londoners, related to Cromwell. The maidens of Lyme, partly by the assistance of the populace and also by connivance of the persons in power, would recover William's remains for burial in Lyme churchyard.

4.   Sampson Larke, a learned and pious dissenting teacher of Lyme, who was about to make a speech, but was interrupted by the guard with the laconic observation that the work of the day being so great, they could not afford him time.

5.   Dr Benjamin Temple, from Nottingham, was the Duke's physician in Holland, who knew nothing about the intention of invading England until they were at sea.

6.   Captain Arthur Matthews who died very heroically, forgiving the executioner but advising him to leave off his bloody trade; who replied, that he was forced to do it against his mind.

7.   Joseph Tyler, a learned Bristol gentleman, who had a command in the Duke's army. He wrote a hymn shortly before he was to die.

8.   William Cox, who was the first man to enlist with the Duke after his landing, and whose two sons, John and Philip, are also condemned [though they would be reprieved and transported to the Caribbean colonies].

9.   Samuel Robins, a Charmouth fisherman, who boarded the Duke's ship to sell his catch. He was then compelled to pilot the vessel into Lyme. Judge Jeffreys would have pardoned him, but for it being proved in court that a subversive book, entitled *The Solemn League and Covenant*, having been found in his house.

10. Josias Ascue, about whom nothing is known.

11. John Madders, Constable of Crewkerne, forwarded news of the Duke's landing to King James II, but then accepted

command of a company in Monmouth's service and would be taken prisoner at the Battle of Sedgemoor. He might have been pardoned, but for the Judge Jeffreys hearing him described as "a good Protestant". Says Jeffreys: "Oho! He is a Presbyterian. I can smell them 40 miles. He shall be hanged."

12.   Captain John Kidd, a man of great courage, beheld the other eleven dead before him, and said it was a dreadful sight. After praying devoutly for some time he seemed comforted and resigned to his fate.

1685   John Holloway appeared in arms at Lyme Regis at the time of Monmouth's landing, in order to oppose him, but not being properly supported he joined the Duke's party. He later surrendered himself in response to the King's proclamation, in order to obtain a pardon, but was a few hours late. As a result he appeared before Judge Jeffreys and was sentenced to hang, with the execution being carried out the same month [September]. He told his guards: "You seem to be brave fellows; but if I were to have my life for fighting the best five of you, I should not question it." John Bennett, a very aged man of Lyme, who was supported by the parish, and which circumstance was mentioned to Judge Jeffreys, he replied that they had no occasion to trouble themselves on that account, for he would ease them of the charge. At the place of execution, his son offered to die in his stead, and actually attempted going up the ladder for that purpose.

1685   William Lancaster of Bridport is another who has been executed. It is said that, just before he was hanged, he prayed for the Duke of Monmouth, who he supposed to be at that time living, notwithstanding the general belief of his death [being beheaded for treason, on the scaffold beside the Tower of London].

1689 – 29 December.   The distinguished physician Thomas Sydenham of Wynford Eagle, north-east of Bridport, has died in his London house, in Pall Mall, after suffering severely from calculus – a hard stony deposit in his organs. His works contain for the first time adequate descriptions of chronic bronchitis, influenza, chorea, scarlet fever, measles and hysteria, as well as the best account of the gout, from which he had suffered since 1649. He noted the periodic and varying occurrences of epidemic diseases and popularised the cooling method for the relief of the smallpox, as well as the use of bark in agues [shivering fevers].

1695   With the publication of his *Compendium Anatomicum*, John Case of Lyme Regis has become London's most famous and fashionable doctor. He has put the following distich above his door: "Within this place Lives Doctor Case."

1695   Edmund Gibson, in the first English translation of William Camden's *Britannia*, writes that Bridport cannot "maintain the name of a port". Gibson adds that "the inhabitants have lately attempted it, and fail'd to in the undertaking: the tides perpetually barring it with sand, against which they could not find any remedy".

1703   Parish registers record an exceptional gale: "The great storm, both at sea and land, the greatest ever man knew in England was on the 26th day of November in the year 1703."

1720   Lace-making has become well established in Dorset, with the main centre of activity at Lyme Regis being an extension of the industry that flourishes around Honiton in south-east Devon. Other Dorset lace-making centres are at Sherborne and Blandford. The latter is in vogue for high-fashion wares, up to £30 a yard and equal to any made in Devon. In particular it is used for steinkirks, the fashionable neckware. Hand-making of lace is a skill requiring great patience.

1741   The Foundling Hospital has been established in Hatton Garden, London, as the first institution in the capital to care for abandoned children. It is funded by Thomas Coram [1668-1751], the son of a Lyme Regis mariner, who became a shipwright and settled in Massachusetts [1694] where he proceeded to build up a fortune. [One of its governors was William Hogarth, whose resoundingly strong portrait painting of Coram is one of the best of its genre in the 18th century. The Thomas Coram Foundation survives and there is an impressive statue to him in Brunswick Square, London WC1. Coram Tower, in Lyme, overlooks the Cobb cliffs from the north side of the Holm Bush car-park.]

1742   A pier has been completed at Bridport, and a small harbour has been built by Kane Williams, but the flow of the river is insufficient to carry away the sand that blocks the inner haven. Ships above 40 tons cannot enter, even at high-water. The entrance is dangerously unprotected in a south-west wind, which blows for much of the time.

1749   The 350-ton Dutch merchantman *Hope* of Amsterdam, a 30-gun treasure ship returning home from the West Indies with a cargo worth £50,000, mainly in gold, encountered tempestuous weather in Lyme Bay on the night of 16 January. It was extremely dark and no light appeared from the lighthouse on Portland. The violent sea stranded the *Hope* on the Chesil Beach, across The Fleet between Fleet House [Moonfleet Hotel] and Langton Herring, where a 400-strong mass from the coastal villages and Portland gathered as dawn betrayed her predicament. They came not to rescue but as a "merciless battalion" that sub-divided into plundering bands each of about 20 in number. "In vain did the captain and his company in faltering foreign accents repeat as well as they could – 'No wreck. The goods ours. Bring it to we and we will pay for it' [meaning the salvage]. The winds and waves showed an equal disregard to this language of distress. The pillaging parties threw all they could snatch in one heap, for the security of which

Portland labourer Augustin Elliott was posted, as commander of an armed select party. As soon as the reflex of the sea had made the ship accessible, the scattered bands again arrived, in a hostile manner, armed with cutlasses, clubs, hooks, and such like. They marched down to the ship swearing it was a wreck and if not so they could make it a wreck. From curses and menaces they proceeded to offer violence and outrage to those persons, whom even the merciless and furious sea had left unhurt. The injury of strangers in distress is adding barbarity to iniquity and committing an act exceedingly sinful in the sight of both God and man."

1751   The *Reine Gabrielle*, laden with more than 5,000 gallons of honey from Dunkirk, was beached by a storm at Bridport on 25 March. Robert Fowler Coade, a Lyme Regis merchant, organised its floating and brought the ship into the harbour at West Bay. All hands and cargo have been saved "and re-shipped entire, without the least embezzlement from the country people, tho' they came down in large numbers to the beach the night the vessel was stranded in hopes of making a prey of both ship and cargo".

1751   Warren Lisle, the commander of a squadron of Excise cutters engaged in the harassment of smugglers, has found influential friends in the Fane family of Lyme Regis, the Earls of Westmorland, who have rewarded his interest with an appointment that is in their patronage. He has been declared Mayor of the town. [For three periods; being 1751-52, 1753-54, and during the early 1760s.]

1751 – 4 December.   Anna Coad[e] writes from Dorchester, on her arrival from London: "I bless God I had a very safe journey, and though met with a Highwayman, yet a kind providence preserved us from being robbed. I caught a great cold on the road, and this air is very sharp at this time of year, which has confined me, ever since I came down, but live in hopes of being better. All friends at Dewlish are well, Mr Cousin Skinner is there. I have not yet been able to get out to pay them a visit, and the roads are too bad for them to travel far; [I] have the pleasure of hearing from [them] twice a week. I am at Mr Jacobs still, not being able to get a house at present." The rest of the letter is taken up with religious verses for a Mr Newman, and "a short meditation against the fears of death". There is also an enquiry about the Lyme Regis appointment of "a minister at Silver Street, [where] there is one Mr Spencer" she chooses to hear preach, "who was brought up under Dr Merriott. I hear he is a serious moderate gentleman." Silver Street has a Baptist Chapel. [Anna Coad, or Ann Coade as she also appears in records, was baptised at Lyme Regis on 27 February 1722. As one might guess from the letter, she would die a spinster, and was buried at Lyme on 16 June 1806.]

1754 – 22 December.   Rev Thomas Francklyn today addressed his sermon preached at the churches of Fleet and Chickerell to the recent occasion of shipwrecks along this coast. He reminded parishioners of the Acts of Parliament relating to ships that are stranded on the shore and in particular the penalties they contain for those that plunder the merchant goods: "This has been long looked upon as a thing right and lawful to be done by them who received it from their forebears, and practised it betimes. And, indeed, nothing can reconcile an act as shocking to anyone's reason and conscience, but the frequency of committing."

1756   The pier and basin at Bridport Harbour have been enlarged, but it remains unsatisfactory in severe weather.

1764 – June.   Such a quantity of mackerel was caught at Abbotsbury as the oldest men living don't remember. There were drawn on shore, by twice shooting seine nets, at least 200,000 fish. Thousands of these are still on the beach, there not being sufficient people to carry them away.

1766 – 1 May.   A dairyman at Long Bredy, in the hills between Bridport and Dorchester, has realised that he made a bad bargain when he agreed in March to produce, for £5, three solid feet of butter for delivery today. He has not performed the agreement, which will probably occasion a law suit.

1767 – 10 August.   Last week three dead bodies were taken up on the shore near Abbotsbury, and one at Portland, with two sides of a boat. The skin was also found of two hands with the nails on. There was a watch and sixpence found on one of the bodies. No account has been received of any vessel lost on this coast.

1767 – 14 December.   It is reliably reported that two young men of Chideock, west of Bridport, have had some words with their sweethearts. They went away together and hanged themselves, both on one tree; but the bough they tied themselves up to broke down before they were quite dead. One of them remained speechless for several days.

1770   Thomas Hollis [1720-74], the admirer of 17th century republican literature who has spent a fortune on books which he has given to the American library at Harvard and those of continental universities including Berne and Zurich, has retired from London to Urless Farm, Corscombe, near Beaminster. Its fields are being given American and libertarian names.

1770   Samuel Hearne [1745-92], the explorer who during the past two years has found the passage through the icy waters along the north-western edge of America for the Hudson's Bay Company, is remembered in Beaminster where he lived as a youth. [His book, *Journey from Hudson's Bay to the Northern Ocean*, would be published posthumously, in 1795].

1774   Thomas Hollis died on 1 January and has been buried, with his horse it is said, in a field at Urless Farm, Corscombe [see

1700]. He has lived as a recluse in a frugal manner, abstaining from intoxicating liquors, spices, salt, butter, and milk. His estates have been left to his friend Thomas Brand of The Hyde, Ingatestone, Essex, who now styles himself T. Brand Hollis. [Brand Hollis died in 1804, leaving both estates to the Unitarian clergyman Dr John Disney].

1772   The decline in the cloth trade, lost to the new manufactories in the North, and a requirement for ships larger than those that can be built at Lyme, has caused a grave depression in the west of Dorset. A total of 118 houses have fallen into decay and replaced by hovels. There is no white bread, the shelves of shops are empty, and the daily labouring wage has fallen to fourpence.

1770s   The Revenue cutter *Sherborne*, commanded by Lieutenant John Cartwright [1740-1824] is operating from Lyme Regis in an extension of the sea-war that rages with vast quantities of spirits and luxury goods continuing to be smuggled into the West Country.

1784   Warren Lisle [1699-1788], the retired Grand-Master of Customs and Excise, has returned to Lyme Regis, at the age of 84, in order to try and wrestle from the town's powerful Fane family their traditional Parliamentary seat. They were his former associates. He looks back with some sadness on his otherwise exemplary career, as the most successful maritime commander in the service, which has terminated on this divisive note because he was "too honest about the fraudulent practices in the various ports".

1788 – 13 March.   It is reported from Stoke Abbott, west of Beaminster, that Charles Tyte – "a gormandiser" – has consumed 133 eggs in an hour, plus a large piece of bacon and a quantity of bread. He then complained that he had not eaten a full supper.

1788   Earlier in the year the Clarendon Press at Oxford published anonymously the romantic poem *Lewesdon Hill* which describes a May morning climb to the top of the wooded summit near Broadwindsor and the delightful prospect and its associations. There has been such national acclaim for this harmonious blank verse that a second edition has been printed, which identifies its author as William Crowe [1745-1829], the rector of Stoke Abbott, near Beaminster. [It was praised by Tom Moore for imagery "of the highest order" and by Samuel Rogers for "noble passages"; Wordsworth, Coleridge and Bowles also acknowledged it as an important contribution to the Romantic Movement.]

1789 – August.   The brig *Endeavour*, sailing up-Channel from Sidmouth en route to Newcastle, where she was to take on board a cargo of coal, has been driven ashore near Bridport Harbour. Her departure coincided with a storm. The crew were eventually saved.

1791 – 31 January.   On Friday last, 28 January, a passenger on the top of the *Western* coach, bound for Exeter, died of exposure from the cold, between Chideock and Charmouth. He had been taken sick at Chideock, from the excessive cold of the foregoing night, but expired before reaching the next stop, and was removed at Charmouth.

1792   An increasing volume of trade is passing through Bridport Harbour, which is now able to take vessels of 300 tons. Considerable quantities of flax are imported from Russia and consumed in the town's cordage and netting industry. Lumber arrives from Norway, Prussia, and North America, and grain also from across the Atlantic. Some eight vessels from the port, each of about 100 tons, operate around this country and to Norway.

1794   There are now 11 coasting vessels, representing a total of above 950 tons, operating this year from Bridport Harbour.

1795 – 17 November. Rear-Admiral Sir Hugh Cloberry Christian [1747-98] yesterday set sail from Spithead, outward bound into a wind that became a hurricane. They were tasked to sail to the West Indies, where Sir Hugh is to be Commander-in-Chief, but few of the vessels reached a point between Portland and Bridport, and none any further. The flagship, the 98-gun *Prince George*, limped back to Portsmouth with her rigging smashed and almost unseaworthy beyond repair. The less fortunate craft foundered or were driven ashore and 1,000 men are estimated to have drowned. Two hundred bodies have been picked up along the Chesil Beach.

1797 Dr George Mitford, who moved into the Great House [45-48 Broad Street] at Lyme Regis last year, has found great fortune through the national lottery. He insisted on obtaining ticket numbered 2224 on the instructions of his daughter, Mary Russell Mitford [1787-1865], who was emphatic about the matter as the figures add up to her age. A short time later the counterpart was drawn and they found themselves better off by £20,000. [Though Dr Mitford, as an incorrigible gambler, would proceed to squander it, and was eventually saved from penury by publication of *Triumph of Temper*, written by that precocious ten-year-old.]

1803 Richard Roberts has erected beside the River Bride at Burton Bradstock [Mill House] the first flax swingling mill in the West of England. This works in a horizontal mode, the Bridport-imported flax being held against the edge of a board at openings in the frame. There it is struck by the scutchers – pieces of wood which project from a vertical shaft that revolves swiftly. This process smashes the stalks and thereby separates them from the flax.

1803 – 5 November. Bonfire Night will be an anti-climax at Lyme Regis after a fire earlier today destroyed 42 houses. It started at Crossman's Bakery in Monmouth Street and was immediately fanned by gale-force winds into an inferno that devastated the Coombe Street area and extended northwards to the Mill Green cloth factory, opposite the Angel Inn.

1804 – September. Having stayed at Lyme Regis last November, where she witnessed a huge fire, Miss Jane Austen [1775-1817] has returned to the town with her family who have taken rooms at Hiscott's Lodging House in Broad Street [demolished and replaced by the new Three Cups in 1807]. She writes of a walk from the Assembly rooms, up the Bell Cliff steps and along the unlit Middle Row alley, above the Shambles, to the lodgings: "The ball last night was pleasant but not full for Thursday. My father stayed contentedly till half past nine (we left a little after eight) and then walked home with James and the lanthorn, though I believe the lanthorn was not lit, as the moon was up, but this lanthorn may sometimes be of great convenience to him. [Her tart view of Lyme society was developed for the novel *Persuasion*, published posthumously, in 1818.]

1805 A west Dorset man has become a national hero. Admiral Sir Samuel Hood [1762-1812] served with great distinction under Lord Nelson at Santa Cruz [1797], and in command of the *Zealous* at the Battle of the Nile, and now off Rochefort, where he has lost his right arm [25 September 1805]. The son of purser Samuel Hood and his wife Anne of Kingsland, Netherbury, near Beaminster, he returned to Dorset as MP for Bridport. [He would be back on active service when he died of a sudden fever, in Madras, as Commander-in-Chief of the East Indies. HMS *Hood*, the 42,100-ton battlecruiser sunk by the *Bismarck* in 1941, was named for him.]

1805 A ship-builder's yard has commenced business at a site on the west side of the inner pool at Bridport Harbour. Several slips slope into the water. [This was immediately south-west of the present West Bay harbour, on the west side of the channel that now leads to the sea.]

1806 – May. The Admiralty Shutter Telegraph System between London and Portsmouth has been extended westwards to Plymouth. The Plymouth Line has been built by George Roebuck to Lord George Murray's design in the months since the Battle of Trafalgar [21 October 1805], despite all the difficulties of weather and terrain. Lookouts with telescopes watch the next stations in the line and on a clear day the warning of invasion or instructions to the Fleet can be passed by shutter-signals between the Admiralty and Plymouth in less than an hour. There are nine stations that span the centre of Dorset, being from east to west at Pistle Down, Chalbury, Blandford Racecourse, Bell Hill [Belchalwell], Nettlecombe Tout, High Stoy, Toller Down, Lambert's Castle, and Dalwood Common [since transferred to Devon].

1810 Miss Mary Anning, the Lyme Regis fossil hunter, has sold the remains of a large antediluvian "Fish-Lizard" to the owner of Colway Manor, for £23. Its bones had been washed out of the cliffs by a storm. [This ichthyosaurus is now in the British Museum (Natural History)].

1814 – 15 January.   The weather is greater in severity than anyone can remember for 40 years. The roads are many feet deep with snow and the mails from London required a chaise and four horses, arriving in Exeter from Dorchester some 18 hours after the usual time. In Devon, a soldier was found dead at Haldon with £21 in his pocket; nearby were three members of the Renfrew Militia, also dead, and their bodies have been conveyed to Chudleigh. From elsewhere in the country comes news of deaths from exposure to the extreme cold. Seven boys were drowned on the Trent, by the breaking of the ice, on which they had imprudently ventured before it was sufficiently strong.

1814 – 26 October.   George Hellier, a 37-year-old patten maker of Allington, near Bridport, was discharged today from Dorchester Castle gaol for the *Laurel* hulk at Portsmouth and passage to New

South Wales. He was sentenced to death at the summer Assize in Dorchester, for horse stealing, but this was commuted to transportation for life. He leaves behind a wife and three children.

1817 – 20 January.　Two wine-laden vessels have been lost off the west Dorset coast in last night's storm. Only one man was saved from the *Trois Amis* of Bordeaux which was foundered near West Bay and an unidentified chasse-marree is a total loss on Charmouth beach with all hands being drowned.

1818　A Roman tessellated pavement has been discovered near Halstock, John Bellamy writes in the Gentleman's Magazine: "I visited this pavement yesterday, about four miles from my house, having set out with the full intention to have taken a drawing for you immediately, when an event prevented me that I should most certainly have anticipated; the frost setting in severely deprived me of the natural animation necessary to complete my purpose."

1819 – September.　A smallpox epidemic has spread through Bridport, killing 26.

1819　An engraving by George Cruikshank [1792-1878] that was published in London on 8 September shows the bathing machines on the beach beside the Cobb harbour at Lyme Regis, with the ladies, as is the custom, taking the water without a costume between them. The title "Hydromania ! or a Touch of the Sub-Lyme and Beautiful" is satirical, being a comment both upon the unfathomable fashion for cold water and Edmund Burke's essay *On the Sublime and Beautiful.*

1820　Lyme Regis fossil collector Mary Anning has sold a fine antediluvian "Fish-Lizard" to the Duke of Buckingham for 120 guineas. [This being a splendidly preserved ichthyosaurus.]

circa 1820   The death has taken place at Belmont House, Lyme Regis [now the home of John Fowles], of Mrs Eleanore Coade who manufactured Regency terracotta mouldings, known as Coade Stone, for decorative wall-facings. The technique is variously said to have been developed by George Coade, who died in 1769, or by Mrs Coade's father. Mrs Coade expanded the business after her husband's death and built Belmont House incorporating this product. She claimed for it "a property peculiar to itself of resisting the frost and consequently of retaining the sharpness in which it excels every kind of stone sculpture". These products [larger and later items carrying the firm's name "COADE LAMBETH"] are made in the family business based at Pedlar's Acre on London's South Bank. At Lyme, set into the Ware Cliffs between Devonshire Head and Monmouth Beach, she established Lyme Cement Works, to make hydraulic cement, being a specialist product for use in harbour-works, having the capacity to harden under water. [The best known public specimen of Coade Stone is the big statue of a red lion that sits on the east end of Westminster Bridge, beside the County Hall site of Coade's Gallery, which was the firm's showroom. He was formerly one of the mascots of the Lion Brewery, which was demolished for the building of the Royal Festival Hall, in 1950.]

1821   Chilcombe residents have insisted that there is no public trackway across their parish. They are objecting to others using the road through the centre of the parish, over the hills from Askerswell to Puncknowle. They write: "We the undersigned householders, farmers dwelling in the parishes adjoining the parish of Chilcombe, do declare and make known to whomsoever it does concern that there is not nor ever was to our knowledge a public wagon or cart road through any part of the parish of Chilcombe. And in order to prevent as much as we can any legal claim to that effect we have set our hands this 3rd September 1821." [This is still an unclassified County Council maintained public road, though a short gated section on the slope between

Chilcombe and Rudge Farm was not tarred until the 1950s. There is a quarter mile spur from it, also maintained by the council, into the hamlet of Chilcombe. The main purpose of the objection was to prevent the through route being diverted along this second track and then out from the cluster of buildings on the other side. In this they were successful, and it remains an idyllic cul-de-sac.]

1822   The Plymouth Line of Admiralty Telegraph Stations [see 1806] has been converted to the simpler semaphore system, replacing the shuttered arrangement, which was devised by Sir Home Riggs Popham and adopted by Parliament in 1814. Thomas Goddard began the survey for these changes in 1818 and Henry Maudsley of Lambeth were contracted to supply the equipment, with telescopes by Dolland, but the system did not come into operation until this year. A new survey was announced on 15 April that will lead to an entirely different line of semaphore stations to replace the existing locations.

1823   Rook pie is a popular Dorset delicacy but in a case reported from the Maidstone Assizes, Mr Baron Graham expressed doubts that anyone would eat the birds, and said he had never heard of a rook pie. The Weymouth Gazette commented on 24 August: "The good folk in the West of England will be amused by reading this; a strong stomach to encounter a rook pie? If Mr Baron Graham should ever happen to pass through Dorchester when young perchers are beginning to caw, we would engage to provide him with a rook pie equal, if not superior, to any powdered pigeon reared in the kingdom of Cockaigne."

1824   The cliffs near Lyme Regis have yielded a perfectly preserved fossilised Dimophodon, typical of the creatures which inhabited the Earth before The Flood. It has been reassembled and is being offered for sale by Miss Mary Anning. [This dinosaur is now known as a pterodactyl.]

1824   A new harbour has been built at Bridport, as a rectangle dug in the marshes of the parish of Bothenhampton, between Mr Good's Ship Yard and the Rope-walk and the premises on the eastern side of the estuary of Messrs Gundry and Ewens. It has now been linked to the sea by a channel to the west of the Bridport Arms Inn and the Revenue Watch House. A crane house has been built on the east side of this run, to the north-west from the inn. The civil engineer is Mr James Green and the work has been carried out under the supervision of Mr Francis Giles. Upwards of 200 men have been working each day for many months and it is estimated that the total cost will be £41,800.

1824   Storm-force winds coinciding with a high tide on the evening of 22 November caused the raging sea to break over the top of the Chesil Beach, inundating and destroying much of the coastal villages of Chesil [Chiswell at Portland] and westwards at Fleet. Even on the eastern-facing shores the sea did considerable damage and washed away the Weymouth esplanade. The Wyke Regis parish register records: "This day will ever be memorable for the dreadful catastrophe which caused such destruction along the whole western coast. The village of Chesil was nearly destroyed, 26 of the inhabitants drowned, and upwards of 80 houses damaged or washed down by a tremendous surf which broke over the Chesil bank and bore everything away with irresistible violence; there blew a most dreadful hurricane such as never had been before in the memory of man. At 9 o'clock a most horrid scene presented itself. The sea ran down the streets of Chesil with sufficient depth of water to float a vessel of 100 tons and the wrecks of houses and the furniture of the poor inhabitants were everywhere strewn on the shore. The ferry house leading to Portland was washed away and the ferryman drowned. Three quarters of the esplanade at Melcombe [Regis] was entirely thrown down ... the waves of sea washed over the high old road and filled all the lower parts of the houses in Gloucester Row and The Crescent with gravel and water ... The same storm destroyed the church at Fleet and threw down several houses but fortunately no lives were lost. The *Colville*, a West Indiaman of 400 tons, was wrecked in the West Bay [off Portland] and every soul on board perished.

1824 – December. *Ebenezer* is the ship that is the talk of the Dorset coast, having achieved a unique claim to fame, by sailing up the English Channel without having passed south of Portland Bill. Instead the 95-ton sailing vessel, a Government sloop carry stores for the Royal Navy, was left stranded on top of the Chesil Beach by the Great Gale [22 November]. She has now been tugged down the inland-facing side of the unstable pebble bank and re-launched at high tide into a specially dug trench that saw her safely into the backwater and Portland Roads. From this anchorage she made ready, and resumed her voyage, from Plymouth to Portsmouth.

1825   Refitted at Lyme Regis shipyard last year, after being damaged in last year's great storm, the *Unity* has been dashed to pieces on the beach below the cliffs at Charmouth.

1825 – 15 October.   Captain Sir Richard Spencer [1779-1839] of the Royal Navy, who served under Nelson and retired to 6 Cobb Road, Lyme Regis, has been experimenting to improve the buoyancy of ships' lifeboats, by using several airtight cases made of thin sheet-copper and encased in deal. These were put to the test today at the Cobb. Six cases were fixed to a four-oared galley. Its plug was then removed as eight men stood on the gunwale. They jumped into the sea and then swam back to the craft when it continued to float. All scrambled into her with perfect safety.

1826   Rebuilding of the ancient Cobb harbour at Lyme Regis, badly damaged in the great storm of November 1824 has been completed in 19 months, at a cost of £17,337-0s-9d which is £2,000 below the estimate.

1827   A visitor to Bridport on a Sunday might wonder why the sides of the streets are so far apart, particularly as there is no evidence of cattle or market stalls. The answer that appears on the Monday morning is the home-spinning of yarn for netting, which requires a great deal of space. The paths are known as rope walks.

1831 – September.   The line of Admiralty Semaphore Stations has been completed across Hampshire to Woodfield Green but those planned to take it through Dorset, at Rushmore, Badbury Rings, Bere Regis [Woodbury Hill], Puddletown Heath, Winterbourne Steepleton [Black Down], Coombe [Chilcombe Hill], and Filcombe Hill [Golden Cap], are not to be proceeded with on grounds of prohibitive expense. Experiments are being made with the new Electric Telegraph system.

1832   Lyme Regis has been disfranchised, along with 55 other so-called "rotten boroughs" under "Schedule A" of the Reform Act. The town will no longer return two members to Parliament, as has been its right for more than 650 years.

1832   Cholera outbreaks in Dorset are claiming lives, with 19 of varying ages dying in Bridport at the end of the summer.

1833   Sixteen-year-old Sylvester Wilkins was hanged at Dorchester on Saturday 30 March, for arson at Bridport. This is another achievement for the hanging judge Sir Joseph Littledale. He was such a light boy that weights cast in lead, inscribed with the word "MERCY", were attached to his feet to hasten the execution [being now preserved in Dorset County Museum].

1833   Captain Sir Richard Spencer [1779-1839] of Lyme Regis has left England on HMS *Buffalo* to become the first Government Resident at King George Sound, on the other side of the world. [Which became the harbour and settlement of Albany, in the new colony of Western Australia. His farmstead there is now preserved as The Old Farm, Strawberry Hill, by the National Trust of Australia. "There is no such climate in the world," he wrote home in 1836. "Everything which grows in England comes to perfection here. I have Malta blood oranges growing here before my window on a tree which I brought from the island in 1817. I have eaten grapes, raspberries, currants, and gooseberries from cuttings I brought from my garden in Lyme Regis." Spencer's demise epitomises the gulf between English traditions and Australian informality. "Button your epaulettes!" he told two scruffy sailors whom he summoned to attention in Albany's main street. "Button your mouth!" one of them replied. This threw Sir Richard into a near-fatal cardiac arrhythmia which would keep him in bed for the next two years. He was finished off by a second massive stroke on 24 July 1839 and is buried on the hillside above his farm and the harbour.]

1833 – 31 July. The 752-ton steam-packet HMS *Messenger* has towed the royal yacht *Emerald* from Weymouth to Lyme Regis in order to meet Princess Victoria [1819-1901, Queen from 1837] who is being escorted over the hills by the Earl of Ilchester's Yeomanry, from his lordship's family seat at Melbury House, having spent two nights there. The 14-year-old Princess and her mother, the Duchess of Kent, are on a tour of the South Coast.

1833 – 2 August. People flocked into Lyme Regis from the countryside to assemble together in one dense mass on the Cobb, to watch Princess Victoria's carriage drive at a slow pace along the sands. Having mounted on to the western causeway, the royal party was greeted by the Mayor, John Hussey, who advanced through a double file of Coastguards. The Princess and her mother were then conducted by the Mayor to their place of embarkation, the old Crab Head of the Cobb. A barge was moored at a floating stage to take them to the *Emerald*. The royal carriages were also put on board in the same way. Meantime, to complete the memorable hour, every available boat in the harbour was plying for hire, and filling with onlookers at a shilling a head. It was at 15.00 hours that anchors lifted and the vessels were under weigh, with HMS *Messenger* towing *Emerald* with incredible swiftness. They turned westwards into Lyme Bay and are heading for the naval dockyard at Plymouth.

1834 – 21 August. The *Jane*, a schooner that will be registered in Limerick, has been launched at West Bay. Her displacement is 200-tons.

1834 – 31 December. The customs duties collected for the year at Bridport Harbour totalled £6,364, which is a record for this port. [It was never to be broken.]

1835 In a manner normally reserved for marking royal commemorations, the name "Reform Place" has appeared on buildings in Bridport's north-west suburb of Allington. The Reform Act has widened Parliamentary representation to an enlarged male electorate. What the stone has in common, however, with the majority who celebrate royal events is that it is in a working class area. As the Boundary Commission, which came to re-draw the constituency maps in the wake of the expansion of the electorate, noted about Bridport: "The chief trade arises from the manufacture of hemp and flax, and Allington appears to be the resort of the poorer classes of the population engaged in these manufactures."

1837 Smallpox again causes an epidemic at Bridport, killing 66 people in six months.

1837 Jack Rattenbury, who was born in Beer, Devon [1778], and smuggled for four decades in and around Lyme Regis, has published his *Memoirs of a Smuggler* which records the following courtroom dialogue: "Lawyer Bompass – 'You have kept school at home, and trained up your son?' Rattenbury – 'I have always trained him up in a regular and honourable way, learnt him the Creed, the Lord's Prayer, and the Ten Commandments.' Bompass –

'You don't find there, Thou shalt not smuggle?' Rattenbury – 'No,
but I find there, Thou shalt not bear false witness against thy
neighbour.' Bompass – 'Nobody smuggles now-a-day?' Rattenbury
– 'Don't they, though [to laughter].

1838 – 1 December.   Severe gales over the past 48 hours have
left wreckage and bodies along much of the Chesil Beach. *Le Jean
Bart*, a French smack, was lost near West Bay. A schooner, *Mary
Ann*, has been driven on to the beach at Abbotsbury. Eastwards, the
losses are *Arethusa*, off Fleet (no survivors); *Louise*, a Swedish
barque, wrecked at Wyke; *Columbine*, a schooner, nearby (no
survivors); *Dove*, a Weymouth sloop, abandoned in Chesil Cove;
and *Marie Louise*, a French brig, on the other side of Portland, being
a total loss in Bowleaze Cove.

1839   Eight vessels have been driven on to the Chesil Beach in a
south-westerly gale, with the loss of all on board, but a ninth ship
had a miraculous escape. The force of the waves, at the height of the
storm, threw this 500-ton vessel on to the very top of the beach.
There she rested, high and dry, as the winds abated.

1839 – July.   The double murder scandal at Powerstock has
ended with the suspect, animal doctor John Hounsell, being
acquitted at the Summer Assizes in Dorchester, through lack of
evidence. The bodies of his late wife and the husband of Elizabeth
Gale, who had died in the hamlet of Nettlecombe over the winter,
were exhumed from Powerstock churchyard and subjected to post
mortem on the altar of St Mary's parish church [20 February 1839]
after the vicar, Rev George Cookson, became suspicious. The
surviving spouses had asked him to publish the banns for their
marriage. An inquest was held at the Three Horseshoes alehouse.
Six times the lethal dose of arsenic was found in Mrs Hounsell's
body. It took three weeks for the smell of decomposition to clear
from the church, sufficiently for services to held again. [John and
Elizabeth then left the district and married.]

1839 – 20 September.   The death has occurred of Vice-Admiral Sir Thomas Masterman Hardy, companion in battle and favourite captain of the greatest of all naval heroes, Lord Nelson. The second son of Joseph Hardy, of Portesham, he was born in Martinstown, on 15 April 1769. It would be in his arms that Nelson would die, having achieved the destruction of the French and Spanish fleets off Cape Trafalgar. Mr Beatty, HMS *Victory's* surgeon, and Dr Scott, the chaplain, have both confirmed Nelson's dying words: "Kiss me, Hardy." His Flag Captain went on to the Governorship of Greenwich Hospital, being appointed on 6 April 1834, where he did much to improve the lot of the 2,000 naval pensioners who live in the hospital and Royal Naval College. He has died in the Second Sea Lord's house at Greenwich and his coffin will lie in the dining room before burial in Greenwich Mausoleum.

1844 – 11 May.   The George Inn at Lyme Regis, formerly the town's principal hostelry which had accommodation for a large number of pack-horses, has been consumed by a great fire. It was often visited by the curious, on account of the Duke of Monmouth having set up his headquarters there, after landing at Lyme on 11 June 1685.

1844   A regatta has been held at West Bay. It is the first such event in these parts.

1846   In all the sum of £609-15s has been raised by the public subscription initiated among the Dorset gentry to commemorate the distinguished life of Vice-Admiral Sir Thomas Hardy [see entry for 20 September 1839]. A Gothic column has been built on Black Down, between the Hardy family's homes at Martinstown and Portesham, which has been designed by Arthur Dyke-Troyte. The first stone was laid by Mrs Floyer, wife of John Floyer, MP for Dorset and High Sheriff of the county. The contract price to Mr Goddard, the builder, was £375-19s-6d; opening quarries at Portesham and quarrying stone, £111-13s-3d; to Mr Glegg and Mr H. Barnes for submitting designs, £5 each; advertisements for

donations, £33-10s-11d; for beer £6-1s-8d and £2-19s-8d for
bread and cheese, for the work people on the occasion of laying the
foundation stone in 1844. The base of the tower is at 833 feet
above the level of the sea, to an octagonal design which inclines like
the batter of a mediaeval castle, into parallel sides with a flared top
for the viewing platform. Here the building itself is now 72 feet,
making a total height of 905 feet. A circular staircase winds up the
middle, around the central pillar, and sparsely lit by narrow slit-
windows. From its prominent position it may be seen in every
direction, and in clear weather at a considerable distance, from the
Isle of Wight eastwards and from the Start Point and Dartmoor
westward. It is also a conspicuous object to vessels passing up and
down the English Channel, as well as to all the surrounding
country.

1847 – 9 March. The death has taken place in her home town of
Lyme Regis of the fossil hunter Mary Anning [1799-1847]. She
retrieved the bones of antediluvian "Fish-Lizards" from the cliffs
and beaches around Lyme. [These now being known as dinosaurs,
with her finest specimens being a spectacular ichthyosaurus, found
in 1810, and a perfect pterodactyl, in 1824. Mary Anning is
buried in the churchyard, on the north side of the nave, and would
be commemorated by a stained glass window, partly financed by
members of the Geological Society of London. Memories in Lyme
were of an inoffensive little old lady – but that is pure sexism. She
was assertive enough to tell the king of Saxony: "I am well known
throughout the whole of Europe." The Germans always took more
interest in fossils than the English, as they do to this day.
Interminable scientific arguments fascinated Miss Anning: "I do so
enjoy an opposition among the big wigs."]

1848   There are now 26 ships registered at the port of West Bay,
amounting to a total of 2,465 tons. This is the greatest number of
ships and the largest tonnage to be recorded from the port. [It was
not to be exceeded.]

1849   Franz von Listz, the Hungarian piano virtuoso, has visited Britain and given recitals at Weymouth and Lyme Regis. He is living with Prince Sayn-Wittgenstein in Weimar and composing his symphonies [He joined the Franciscan order in 1865.]

1851 – 26 December.   The barque *Heroine*, outward-bound from London with emigrants for Port Philip Bay, Australia, was driven inshore by storm-force winds and struck rocks near the Cobb at Lyme Regis. She soon became a spectacular wreck. All 44 passengers and crew were saved, in the vessel's own long-boat and a smaller rowing boat, but there was tragedy for the Revenue cruiser *Frances*. One of her boats had been directing the *Heroine*'s boats to the safety of the harbour entrance, but it was overwhelmed by the huge surf and four of the five men were drowned. Three were attached to the *Frances* and the other was the mate of a schooner, the *Honiton Packet*. The survivor was William Bridle, the master of the Primrose cutter.

1852 – 15 January.   Captain Horner's schooner, the *Mary Ann*, of Lyme Regis, was wrecked today on the beach immediately east of the Cobb harbour.

1852 – 26 December.   Bound for Australia, the émigré ship *Heroine* has sunk in Lyme Bay. Though all her passengers and crew were saved it has been at an appalling cost to the people of Lyme Regis, who end this Christmas with the loss of four of their seamen in the otherwise successful rescue.

1853   The *Speedy* has been launched at Bridport Harbour. Her keel is 182 feet and at 1,460 tons she is the largest ship to be built at Good's Shipyard. The owners will register her in Liverpool.

1853 – September.   A lifeboat has been provided at Lyme Regis by the Royal National Institution for the Preservation of Life from Shipwreck, with two thirds of its cost having been raised locally by public subscription. It is an eight-oared Peake-type vessel of 27 feet that is self-righting.

1854 – 7 January.   The Lyme Regis lifeboat was launched after a distress flag was sighted on a brigantine about five miles out in Lyme Bay. Eight Coastguards and four seamen crewed the rescue vessel as she rowed into a south-westerly gale. It was some considerable time before they could reach the *Jeune Rose,* of Bayonne. They found an exhausted crew who had all but lost their battle to control a vessel that was tossing from side to side with its hold almost full of water. The deck cargo was heavy barrels of rosin. Seven lifeboatmen boarded her and almost saved the situation, repairing rigging and setting new sails, as well as pumping out water. The brigantine attempted to tack towards Lyme. Then a particularly heavy squall rolled her on her beam-ends, as barrels broke loose, and the main sail and boom entangled with the lifeboat on her lee side. This caused it to capsize, with two of the five men on board jumping clear, and Coxswain Boxhall and two others were trapped underneath. They were unable to struggle clear for more than 20 minutes – when the brigantine partially righted herself – and then cut away the sails and rigging to enable the lifeboat to be righted. It then took on board both crews, with the exception of Coastguard John Martin who had been drowned when he leapt from the lifeboat, and sailed back to Lyme.

1855 – 5 May.   The proposed Bridport and Maiden Newton Railway, a junction with the Wilts, Somerset and Weymouth line which is in the course of construction, has been incorporated in the Bridport Railway Act which had an unopposed Parliamentary passage. The line will be built by the Bridport Railway Company which is considering a contract from Kenneth Mathieson who estimates its cost at £65,000.

1856 – August.   Three men were in a boat that capsized off Lyme Regis. William Calloway, who was alone in his own boat at

the time, came to their rescue and jumped in the water. He was able
to saved two of the men but the third was swept away by the strong
currents and drowned.

1857 – 9 October. Shortcomings with the Bridport branch
railway have been reported by Captain Tyler of the Board of Trade.
Authorisation for the opening of the line will be delayed until they
are rectified.

1857 – 12 November. Today, Thursday, at 9 am the first train
steamed into Bridport, thereby opening the broad-gauge branch
line from Maiden Newton, via Powerstock. The single track
railway runs for nine and a quarter miles. Its operational use was
sanctioned yesterday by the Board of Trade. There was no time to
arrange a proper welcome but the town will celebrate next
Tuesday with a general holiday and a banquet at the Bull Hotel.
The operating licence for the line has been awarded by its
owners, the Bridport Railway Company, to the Great Western.

1860 A new and larger Peake self-righting lifeboat has been
provided at Lyme Regis. It is 30-feet in length and has been
manufactured by Semmens of Penzance.

1860 – 19 August. Following an overnight gale, when dawn
coincided with high tide, the Lyme Regis lifeboat was launched at
04.00 hours to go to the assistance of a vessel anchored perilously
close to the Chesil Beach, in the vicinity of West Bexington. It took
four and a half hours, during which waves were continually
breaking over her, for the lifeboat to make contact with the
endangered craft, which turned out to be the Dorset brig *Ceres*. She
had been disabled by the loss of sails and her foretopmast. Repairs
were effected and in moderating weather in the early afternoon the
lifeboatmen and crew weighed one another and slipped another.
They limped slowly westwards and at 19.00 hours made the safety
of Bridport Harbour.

1860 – 14 November. The Lyme Regis lifeboat was launched this evening into a full gale that was pounding the locally-owned smack *Elizabeth Ann*, loaded with coal, on to rocks beside the wall of the Cobb harbour. Much careful manoeuvring was necessary before the three Lyme seamen on board could be rescued; just minutes before their stricken vessel was totally awash and starting to break-up.

1862 – 21 March. To meet local requests from the small communities in the valley west of Maiden Newton, an additional station was opened today, at Toller Porcorum, on the Bridport branch railway. It is called Toller.

1863 – October. Bridport, Lyme Regis, and the villages of west Dorset shuddered from an earthquake at 03.35 hours on the first Tuesday this month. The rumbling sound was accompanied by a violent shaking of beds, like the passing of a heavy wagon at a short distance, that lasted about two seconds. Some thought that thieves had broken in; others awoke dizzy. The main oscillation was from east to west with a secondary motion of a whirling nature, producing feelings of dazed terror. Strong doors jumped open, from their catches. The shock was most violent at Bridport Harbour, Burton Bradstock, Chideock, Charmouth, and Lyme Regis. In the latter westward communities many thought that their houses were being taken by a landslip. The fright was considerable though a violent shock in the early hours of the morning comes upon a populace deeply removed from the cares of this world. Even a great noise then is only comparable to a horse rearing in the afternoon, it being impossible to gauge the magnitude of the disaster. Inland the effects were less perceptible but along the Dorset coast most awoke in the middle of that night with a vivid impression of shock.

1864 – June. An estimated total of 50,000 fine mackerel were pulled ashore at Chideock and Burton Bradstock early on a

Wednesday morning. They were brought to Bridport and sent off by rail but, for once, there was sufficient for a fair quantity to be sold in the town, as well, at 10 pence per dozen.

1864 – August.   Miss Alice le Geyt, sojourning at Lyme Regis, was rowing a companion in the lee of the Cobb when she heard cries from the shore and realised that two young boys had slipped from the outer breakwater. Miss le Geyt turned her boat into the hostile waters on the other side and used an oar to hold the craft amid the foaming breakers as she and her lady friend hauled the cold and terrified lads on board. [She would be one of only a handful of female recipients of the silver medal of the Royal National Institution for the Preservation of Life from Shipwreck.]

1864   The usual disturbances took place across the county on Bonfire Night. The Fifth of November was marked by a not very creditable demonstration in Bridport. In the presence of many hundreds of people an effigy of a gentleman, who rendered himself obnoxious by his assertion that the town needed a new drainage system, was burnt in a field at the bottom of South Street.

1865   Skimmington riding is still prevalent deep in the west Dorset countryside. This carnival of anger takes place to show communal disgust at behaviour that has offended against the moral code. The Western Gazette reported from Melbury Osmond on a Monday night in November that "this usually quiet little place was much excited by men and boys parading to the music of tin kettles, tin whistles, also frying pans, etc. It was ascertained that a married farmer had been misbehaving himself. Effigies were intended to be burnt, but the police stopped it. [Nor was this the last example of the custom that Thomas Hardy was to bring into his novel *The Mayor of Casterbridge*, which he started in 1884. Lucy Taylor of Stalbridge, 1879-1947, remembered seeing a procession of local people disguised with sacking over their heads and beating saucepans with tongs and spoons. They escorted a conveyance with caricatures of the guilty pair. These effigies were burnt at The Ring, the village green. The following day no one in Stalbridge was prepared to admit knowing who had taken part in the event.]

1865   Lace-making has died out in Dorset and is suffering hard times in its traditional major centres in the south-east Devon towns. It is now made by machine at Tiverton.

1865   Four buildings have been destroyed by fire at the West Bay shipyard.

1865 – September.   On Tuesday nearly 20 houses were destroyed by fire at Evershot. A hundred people are homeless. The fire devastated Summer Lane, the narrow thoroughfare leading off the main street, uphill towards Cattistock, where only one or two detached cottages remain. The fire started at one o'clock when the back of the carpenter's house was enveloped in flames. These spread to the neighbouring thatched roofs, which were tinder dry as a result of the long drought. Police Constable Hare sent for the two fire engines that are kept at Melbury House but by this time sparks were being blown across the street to the barn and slaughter-house of Trenchard, the butcher. The whole lane became a mass of fire. Telegraphic messages were sent to Yeovil for more engines and to Dorchester for a staff of policemen. Before they arrived the wind changed direction and took the fire into the main street, which also became impassable. So great was the heat that the buildings could not be approached until they had burnt out. There was, however, no loss of life nor even any personal injury sustained.

1865 – September.   There has been another public disturbance of the kind known as skimmington riding in one of the villages on the Somerset border. A story had gained currency in East Coker that the wife of a man who had been in America for two years had been on too friendly terms with a married man in the village, with a result that might have been anticipated. The affair was made all the worse by the fact that both parties were connected with the [Plymouth] Brethren and displayed pretensions to superior sanctity. To show their abhorrence of such cant, some of the inhabitants prepared a couple of effigies which were paraded through the village and burnt in public. The affair created a sensation which is difficult to describe; Coker people will be more than ever suspicious of those who lard their talk with Scripture.

1865 – November.   During the fierce gale of the Monday in the middle of the month, a Cork schooner, the *Black Diamond*, was washed ashore on the West Beach at Bridport and is a total wreck, with the cargo being lost. The whole of the crew were safely landed by means of Manley's apparatus. She was carrying oats, consigned to Mr Knight at the Bull Hotel.

1866 – January.   A hurricane-force blizzard swept through Dorset, Somerset and Devon on the Thursday in the middle of the month. Seventeen ships were blown on to the shore around Portland. Many fine trees were blown over in parks across central Dorset. At Beaminster a lad of 17, who appears to have sat down for a rest, perished of the cold. Eighty-seven ewes in a flock of 470 died on Welcome Hill, Bingham's Melcombe. Not in the remembrance of the oldest person in Rampisham has such a fall of snow come so quickly. Roads for miles around were blocked. Then with the thaw the rise of the stream through the village was equally swift. The carpenter's family near the Tiger's Head had to be rescued from their bedroom window after the water had blocked the staircase. From north Dorset the floodwaters surged into Somerset where the lands around Glastonbury were flooded for miles. Bread had to be delivered from Wedmore in a boat.

1866   The fishermen and boys from the villages along the coast near Weymouth still scour the pebbles of the Chesil Beach for the gold coins that are frequently found washed ashore after a severe gale. There is always considerable excitement when someone picks up the greater part of the value of a week's hard labour as it glistens from between the pebbles. Mostly, we hear, such coins are Spanish, Mexican, or Dutch.

1866 – May. Fire in the chimney of a beerhouse burnt two cottages to the ground at North Allington, Bridport, and the wind conveyed so many sparks across the street that another dwelling opposite shared their fate.

1866 – 11 June. An "initiatory restoration" of Hell Stone cromlech on Portesham Hill, a mile north of the village, has been completed by Rev. Martin Tupper, the author of *Proverbial Philosophy.* Until he started work it was a collapsed burial chamber with a collection of boulders scattered across the highest part of a mound about a hundred feet long. The sarsen stones were partly hidden by earth. The antiquary Charles Warne described the site: "The supports of the capstone have sunk on the south-west side, and are virtually buried by it, its great weight being now chiefly sustained by a single prop on the north side, so that it rests on a greatly-inclined position. It measures more than ten feet in length, about seven feet in breadth, and has an average thickness of at least two feet and a half. Originally it must have rested upon eight or ten supports." However, Mr Tupper's workmen have failed to replace this massive capstone, which now lies on the ground.

1866 – December. Timbers in the relatively new lifeboat at Lyme Regis having been found to have started rotting, the vessel was condemned, and has now been replaced by a larger, 33-feet craft. *William Woodcock* is the gift of an anonymous lady in Manchester. It would not, however, fit into the existing fish-cellar boathouse, so a purpose-built lifeboat house has been provided about 50 yards west of the Cobb.

1867 – 9 January. It was found impossible to launch the new *William Woodcock* from the western beach at Lyme into yesterday's south-westerly gale, which threw a total of five vessels on to the beaches either side of the Cobb harbour. The losses are *Ann and Emily*, *Lyn*, *Maria*, *Spec*, and *Vulcan*. The commander of the Coastguard, Lieutenant W. H. Elton, launched his station galley and crewed it with two of his men and three seamen who volunteered. In fearful conditions they checked each wreck for signs of life and found that three had been empty, on moorings, but two men were on the *Vulcan* and one on the *Maria*. They were all saved.

1867   A new brig, *Dora*, which was launched from Cox's yard at West Bay, has left Bridport Harbour for Cadiz, where she will take in a cargo of salt, and then proceed direct to Newfoundland for fish, with which she will proceed to Brazil. Most of her hands belong to this neighbourhood.

1867 – August.   Fact met fiction at Lyme Regis the other day when the poet Alfred Tennyson [1809-92], staying at Bridport, walked across the western hills to drop in unannounced on the compiler of *The Golden Treasury* anthology, Francis Turner Palgrave [1824-97]. He found his friend in lodgings [Palgrave would buy Little Park in 1872] and demanded, without further ceremony: "Take me to the Cobb and show me the steps from which Louisa Musgrove fell." Miss Musgrove, it will be recalled, is from the pages of Jane Austen. Tennyson has taken rooms at The Three Cups and is considering buying St Mary's, on Trinity Hill, between Lyme Regis and Axminster [though he didn't, moving instead to the Isle of Wight].

1868 – February.   The channel into Bridport Harbour has now been reopened, after being blocked for a fortnight by the wreck of the barque *Marie Leocardie*. She was driven between the piles of the west and east piers at West Bay on 24 January and immediately became a total loss.

1869 – 14 August. Eight Portland quarrymen arrived today on Portesham Hill to complete the task which Rev. Martin Tupper and his workers found impossible, in their "initiatory restoration" of the Hell Stone cromlech. Its capstone, estimated to weigh 16 tons, was left lying on the ground [see entry for 11 June 1866]. With the quarrymen, however, the mission was accomplished in a short time. Having brought screw-jacks they were able to raise it on to the nine upright pillars, which are about five feet above the ground. [The restoration must be regarded as picturesque rather than accurate. The sarsen stones comprised a Neolithic burial chamber dating from between 3500 and 2500 BC.]

1870 – 9 August. The Elementary Education Act has today received the royal assent, to establish the mechanism for basic state education in all parts of the land. The bill was introduced in Parliament on 17 February by W. E. Forster, who was born at Bradpole in Dorsetshire, but had to win through after considerable discussion and much opposition from dissenters.

1872 Loss of life in an imminent shipwreck on a stormy night was averted at Stanton St Gabriel by what local people believe to have been a divine premonition. Isaac Hunter, a Charmouth fisherman, had a violent dream brought on "by anxiety for his lobster pots". He was in such a distressed state that he immediately dressed and set off to run eastwards along the coast for two miles, in the teeth of a gale. He found a French ship in distress, off Golden Cap, and was able to raise the Coastguard and effect the successful rescue of the ship's crew. Their vessel became a total wreck.

1872 Poetry anthologist Francis Turner Palgrave [1824-97] has moved to Little Park, Haye Lane, Lyme Regis. He is best known, indeed already famous, for the *Golden Treasury of the best Song and Lyrical Poems in the English Language* [1861, extended 1897. While living at Lyme he would be appointed Professor of Poetry at Oxford, 1885-95]

1872 – 26 November.   Fourteen men in a ship's boat which was in imminent danger of capsizing in the offshore breakers, were rescued today by the Lyme Regis lifeboat. They had abandoned their vessel, the Shields barque *Cassibelaunus*, when she foundered in the early hours, off Start Point.

1874   The antiquary Charles Warne, in manuscript notes, has recorded the destruction of a major alignment of megaliths about a quarter mile north-east from Hell Stone burial chamber, above Portesham [Ordnance Survey map reference SY 608 869]. "In a small valley, on the down of Portesham Farm, there stood within these last ten years, four upright stones – each about ten feet high – in a line and nearly equidistant from each other, to which was attached the following doggerel: 'Jeffery and Joan, and their little dog Denty, with Eddy alone.' By the direction of the occupier of the farm, Mr Maufield, these stones were removed and built into an adjoining wall. The neighbourhood abounding in stone, one would have thought he could have spared these interesting remains; but what is safe against ignorance and avarice combined."

1874 – June.   The Great Western Railway's Dorset lines, being those from Yeovil to Weymouth and Bridport, will this month be converted from their 7-feet broad gauge to that of the narrower standard track. The lines will be closed for a few days in the middle of the month.

1877   The Portesham Shale Works, sited below Waddon Hill, is sinking a large shaft, the work being carried on day and night by Welshmen and other miners. Two steam engines are continuously at work and the depth now reached is 180 feet.

1877 – 29 May.   John Lothrop Motley [1814-77], the United States Ambassador to London [1869-70] and the world authority on the history of the Dutch Republic and the United Netherlands, has died at Kingston Russell House, where he was staying with the Duke of Bedford.

1879   The shipyard on the west side of West bay has closed, having been forced out of business by the great yards that are making the iron-clads in the North. Bridport Harbour has declined to insignificance during our lifetime, from its thriving trade of the 1830s, and with the arrival of the railway in Bridport town [1857] its demise seemed inevitable. Sailing ships made in the yard are still trading across the oceans, but by the end of the century they will be a memory as well.

1881   The Great Snow began falling on 18 January, deeply and evenly, in quantities larger than anyone can remember. The temperature varied from 25 to 30 degrees Fahrenheit and initially there was not much wind.

1881 – 20 January.   For the past three days and nights Dorset has endured a blizzard with a strong northerly wind driving the snow into every crevice of buildings and piling it across the lanes until it was level with the tops of the hedgerows. Only the railways continue to function and one of the more fortunate of the otherwise cut-off communities is Bradford Abbas where a wagon of coal is being emptied down the embankment for the benefit of villagers.

1881 – 3 February.   The death has taken place, at his home in Charlotte Street, Bedford Gardens, London, of ornithologist John Gould [1804-81]. He was born in Lyme Regis on 14 September 1804 and has the distinction of having discovered and described more birds, in Asia and Australia, than anyone else on Earth. He introduced the budgerigar to England and his 2,999 hand-coloured lithographs of each individual species of bird are rightly regarded as works of art.

1881   Bridport Harbour has ceased to be a bond-port, and the customs duties collected there during its final year are the lowest on record. They total only £1,915.

1881 – 10 December.   *Saladin*, a War Office gas-filled balloon, has drifted out of control and been lost from sight over the sea west of Bridport. Alone aboard is the Member of Parliament for Malmesbury, Walter Powell, who was a guest on the flight. The two crew bounced out of the basket beneath the balloon, which is 60 feet high and 30 feet wide, as it failed to land on cliffs a mile from West Bay. They took off from Bath on the weather research flight at 14.00 hours. *Saladin* floated southwards gathering information on cloud temperatures and humidity for the Meteorological Society. The occupants passed close to Bridport – from where they glimpsed the sea and realised they had underestimated the strength of the northerly wind – and therefore their position, in particular its parlous proximity to Lyme Bay. A desperate attempt was made to make a landing but the balloon basket clipped a coastal pasture at Cliff Close, Eype's Mouth [16.15 hours], throwing out much-needed ballast and two of the three occupants. Captain James Templer was left on the ground, crewman Agg Gardner was pulled 80 feet by a line, breaking his leg. The Member for Malmesbury rose into the evening clouds and floated out across the English Channel.

1882 – 20 January. Wreckage of what is presumed to be the lost British balloon *Saladin* [see entry for 10 December 1881] has been found today on the slopes of Sierra del Piedroza in the mountains of Spain. There were no human remains on board or in the vicinity. [Nothing more was ever heard of Walter Powell MP.]

1882 Fire has destroyed the crane at Bridport Harbour. The crane-house was to the north-east of the Bridport Arms Inn, and the crane used to run on a railway from the end of the east jetty, along the side of the channel, northwards to the harbour. The port's foreign trade ceased last year and it had become the symbol of past prosperity.

1883 The land has been purchased for the extension of the railway from Bridport to the harbour. A tender has been accepted and the cost will be within an earlier estimate of £23,000.

1884 – 31 March. In anticipation of a growing hotel trade the Bridport Railway Company has extended its line, with the aid of £12,000 contributions from the Great Western Railway which holds the operating rights, from the town station to a new terminus by the sea at Bridport Harbour. This station, to be known as West Bay, opened today, with an intermediate station beside the level crossing where the line intersects East Street.

1884 Because of difficulties experienced in launching the lifeboat from its previous location, a new lifeboat house has been built at Lyme Regis. It has cost £500 and stands closer to the harbour.

1884 Pier Terrace has been built near the site of the former crane-house at Bridport Harbour.

1885 Landscape artist Percy Charles Porter [1859-97] of St Pancras has married Bessie Boon of Lyme Regis and is living in the town. [He is buried in Lyme cemetery and two of his smaller works hang in the town's Philpot Museum.]

1887 – 2 April. The funeral took place today of colonial governor Major-General Richard Clement Moody [1813-87] who retired to Lyme Regis. He was the first governor of the Falkland Islands and later served in Canada where the Canadian Pacific Railroad named Port Moody in his honour. He planned the building of New Westminster. General Moody died whilst on holiday at the Bath Hotel, Bournemouth, and has been buried in St Peter's churchyard, Hinton Road.

1887 – 17 July. A letter writer to the Western Gazette reports that the Birmingham Daily Post is carrying regular advertisements for ferns which has been carried away from the roadsides of Dorset in a wholesale manner. The lanes of Dorset, Somerset and Devon are rightly admired for their beauty and it is distressing to see the huge gaps made in them by the fern robbers. These advertisements show the scale of the current demand in the cities for these plants: "Ferns, Ferns, Ferns. – Fifty lovely Devon and Dorset hardy Ferns, 1s. 3d; 150, 3s. 3d." ... "Fifty splendid hardy Dorset Fern Roots, being assorted, well packed in moss and carriage paid, 2s.; one hundred, 3s. 9d."

1888   The Royal Field Artillery has passed through Lyme Regis, slowly up Broad Street, en route to the Dartmoor firing ranges, near Okehampton. Gunners stayed overnight at the [old] Drill Hall [later Marine Theatre] or in private houses throughout the town, with a shilling per head being paid for bed and breakfast.

1889   Lyme's historic fire engine, provided by the Sun Insurance Company in 1710, was able to do little more than damp down the embers after a devastating fire destroyed shops in Broad Street. [From where it went into retirement in the town's Philpot Museum].

1890 – Whit Sunday. A cloudburst over the hills above Lyme Regis resulted in a flash-flood down the River Lim which ripped out stone walls through the lower part of the town. The rainfall in Lyme was 3.7 inches but much more must have fallen towards Lambert's Castle Hill. Rain and thunder around 15.00 hours were followed by sheeting rain and hail from 18.30 to 19.30. The result was that the water level beside the Lynch had risen by 15 feet at dusk. Fortunately, the great surge of floodwater had an easy exit into the sea at low tide, pouring into the Buddle without any resistance. Horn Bridge was also undamaged but a deep gully was torn in the adjoining roadway. Wooden bridges fared worse, being swept away, as were the parapets on Gosling bridge. There followed a busy and beautiful Monday with the torrential rains being followed by bright sunshine.

1890 – 7 November. The Brixham fishing ketch *Rescue*, having lost spars and sails in a gale, was herself rescued today, by the Lyme Regis lifeboat. She was anchored four miles out in Lyme Bay. Lifeboatmen fitted her with their own spare mainsail which enabled her to sail to the Cobb for shelter and repairs.

1891 – 3 March. All roads across the Dorset Downs are blocked by deep snow. There was a report of a man being lost in the blizzard somewhere between Maiden Newton and Sydling St Nicholas. Searchers recovered the body of John Guppy, near Sydling, and Police Constable James Searley has notified the coroner.

1891 Intensely fine powdery snow, carried by a gale which reached Force 10 during the night, blanketed the West Country during the early hours of Tuesday 11 March. The blizzard cut off the western peninsula with huge drifts. Those between Lyme Regis and Honiton are 20 feet high and it is impossible to find the main road. The hurricane veered from north-east to south-east, and during the Tuesday the temperature varied from 29 to 31.5 degrees Fahrenheit but it felt much colder in the strong winds. We hear that the storm centred on Dartmoor, stopping all trains below Okehampton and Plymouth, but the coasts of Devon and Cornwall also shared this indescribably wretched day. A correspondent from Lyme Regis writes: "One of the heaviest snowstorms ever to visit the south of Dorset was experienced at Lyme on Tuesday. The town lies six miles from the nearest railway station, and the only communication is by two well-appointed three-horse 'busses'. On Tuesday the bus, with an extra horse, left the town at nine in the morning, carrying the mails. The conveyance, with great difficulty, reached the high hill known as Hunter's Lodge, where, notwithstanding all efforts, it was found to be impossible to proceed further. The one lady passenger walked to the hotel at Hunter's Lodge, while the driver, Mr Blake, rode back to Lyme

Regis and obtained assistance. By the time the luggage and mails had been transferred to a light wagonette the bus, except for the roof, was invisible, and the roof was only kept clear by the strong winds blowing at the time. Later on the same night, the driver of the mail cart from Illminster to Lyme started to do the journey on horseback, driving being out of the question. On about the same spot as the bus had been buried, the driver lost his horse, and accomplished the rest of the journey on foot, arriving at Lyme at one o'clock on Wednesday morning. Both horse and bus were eventually recovered and the mail carts resumed running on 17 March." On the Sunday following the blizzard the body of a man named Bisgood, a labourer, was found near Offwell. He had not been seen alive after leaving the New Inn, Honiton Hill, on Tuesday evening.

1891 – July.   A 34-feet water-ballast self-righting lifeboat has been issued to Lyme Regis. *Susan Ashley*, named for the donor's late mother, is one of several vessels financed by Charles Carr Ashley of Kingston-on-Thomas.

1891   A golf-links has been opened on the East Cliff between West Bay and Burton Bradstock. [The course of the West Dorset Golf Club].

1895 – 25 November.   The American artist James Abbott McNeill Whistler [1834-1903] who gained notoriety by suing John Ruskin for slander in 1878 and wears his derisory one farthing damages as a watch-charm, has spent a productive 11-week painting holiday in Lyme Regis. He arrived in the town in September with his wife Beatrice (Trixie), for the benefit of her health [she had terminal cancer] though she returned to Chelsea at the end of October. Whistler stayed to finish his portrait of the "Master Smith of Lyme Regis", blacksmith Samuel Govier [1855-1934], and his workplace "The Little Forge, Lyme Regis" [now Woolworths]. He has completed nine pictures in all, including

"Little Rose of Lyme Regis", a portrait of Rose Rendell, the daughter of a former mayor, who was shocked by his offer to paint her as she thought he meant it literally and would cover her body. Another little girl to be painted by the master is Ada Case [1885-1973] who is immortalised as the "Dorsetshire Daisy" and another child is the "Little Yellow Girl" [both paintings lost]. Whistler has been staying at the Red Lion Hotel in Broad Street, though a few days were spent on the other side of the road in the Three Cups Hotel. The lithograph "Sunday – Lyme Regis" shows the street scene looking uphill from outside here. The painter's studio was set up in the upstairs room behind 51 Broad Street which he shared with his companion Arthur Studd [1864-1919], a Leicestershire landscape and portrait artist. Writing to his wife, Whistler comments on the pensive and disturbed nature of his Lyme canvases: "This work may and doubtless will bear witness to the innermost of agonies we have gone through ... how right you were in making us stay here – for if I had gone without carrying these works on – I should have remained in the bitter fog – of indecision and want of pluck." For, he would add, "the one great truth that has impressed itself upon me is that time is an element in the making of pictures and haste their undoing".

1897   The death has been announced of landscape painter Percy Charles Porter [1859-97] who lived at Lyme Regis.

1900 – April.   Subsidence during last winter damaged the 13th-century Purbeck marble shrine to Saint Wite, whose Latinised name is Saint Candida, in the parish church at Whitchurch Canonicorum. It is one of only two such martyr's tombs that have survived in the whole of England, so its displacement and subsequent opening and repair have attracted considerable interest. Inside, on its edge at the north side, there is an oblong leaded reliquary, 29 inches long, inscribed "+ HIC . REQESCT . RELIQE . SCE . WITE." [Here rest the relics of Saint Wite.] It appears to have been opened previously, probably in the 16th century. There is a thigh-bone at the top, 14 inches in length, but the other thigh-bone is missing, in accordance with local tradition [see entry for 1912] and the bones are described as belonging to a small woman apparently of about 40 years of age. She is said by local people to have been killed in a Danish raid on Charmouth, but academics favour the alternative view that she was with Saint Boniface in Germany in 755, when he and 50 of his cohorts were massacred. The martyrdoms were recognised and ordered by Archbishop Cuthbert to be celebrated annually at Whitsuntide, which used to be the case with Saint Wite or Saint Candida, as she was alternatively known, at Whitchurch Canonicorum. [The shrine, with three oval slits, still receives offerings of letters, cards and money, begging for her intercession on behalf of the sick.]

1900   The specimen of *Magnolia campbellii*, the pink tulip tree from Sikkim that was planted in Abbotsbury Castle grounds by the 4th Earl of Ilchester in 1864, has achieved its first flowering. It is now a 30-foot tree. [It was 80 feet high and still flowering in the 1990s; they reach a height of 150 feet in the Himalayas.]

1901 – 1 July.   The Great Western Railway, the operating company of the Bridport branch line, has today bought out the Bridport Railway Company which owned the permanent way. £6 is being paid for each £10 ordinary share.

1901 – 19 July.   When 13-year-old Bill Camplin went tonight to ring the eight o'clock curfew bell in Lyme Regis parish church he had the shock of his life. The body of a retired sexton at St Michael's, 87-year-old John Upjohn, was hanging between the bell-ropes. [Camplin recalled the suicide and his "affrightened lad" notoriety from his Parkstone retirement in 1975: "My father made me go and touch the body so I wouldn't be frightened afterwards. Had he known how many dead I should see in the war he wouldn't have bothered."]

1901   Mr W. Hardy Manfield of Portesham House, representing the descendants of Vice-Admiral Sir Thomas Hardy, has leased the Hardy Monument [see entry for 1846] to the National Trust for Places of Historic Interest or Natural Beauty, which was founded in 1894-95. The landmark was restored in 1900 as a result of initiatives largely funded by Colonel Robert Williams MP, whose seat is Bridehead, in the delightful valley at Littlebredy. It is the Trust's first Dorset property [leasehold, that is; the first freehold property would be the Cerne Giant hill-figure, in 1920].

1901   A convenient early morning service from the East Street station at Bridport to the sea at West Bay has become known as the "Bathing Train". At other times the railway has strong competition, particularly when the shops close early at four o'clock on Thursday afternoons, from the carriage gathered beside the Greyhound and other posthouses.

1902   Lyme Regis has a burning cliff, which is dubbed "The Lyme Volcano" and appears to have come about naturally from the oxidisation of pyrite with the oil shale; a spontaneous combustion that can take place in these rocks. Pyrite contains 53 per cent sulphur. The oily cliffs have also sparked off the last and most determined of the Victorian attempts to discover a Dorset coalfield, though we hear that it is now to be abandoned without result. A year ago a syndicate ignored geological advice and with a team of engineers from South Wales they bored to 1,300 feet before giving up. They were convinced they would find a seam of coal at a depth of some 600 feet. This is the deepest hole ever to be sunk in Dorset. [It would remain so until the onset of oil exploration, in the 1930s. As for the fire, it continued to smoulder through the Edwardian decade, but cynics claimed it was kept going only by surreptitious delivery of cart-loads of coal, courtesy of the town's hoteliers who had no wish to see the life go out of a tourist attraction.]

1903   Curving six miles through the deep-cut valleys of south-east Devon, and bridging the biggest with a great viaduct at

Combpyne, a branch railway has at last been built into Lyme Regis. Its junction with the London and South Western Railway is at Axminster.

1903 – 12 March.   Having struck the west pier of the harbour channel at West Bay, the schooner *Albion* is now a wreck on the beach.

1904 – 8 December.   Mary, Princess of Wales, today visited Lady Stavordale at Abbotsbury. She is staying at the Ilchester Arms.

1908 – 8 September.   The police have sent a warning to Martinstown schoolchildren cautioning them that action will be taken if they continue to throw stones at motor cars.

1912   Relics that have been found recently at Lambeth Palace include a bone with the label: "The thigh-bone of St Candida." This is a Latinisation of the English word white, through what was an erroneous supposition that "Wite" meant white. Saint Wite is the patron saint of the west Dorset church of Whitchurch Canonicorum and she is said to have been with Saint Boniface when he was martyred, with 50 cohorts, on his final mission to Germany, at the massacre at Dorkum near Utrecht on 5 June 755. There was a tradition that one of her thigh bones is missing from the shrine at Whitchurch, verified when it was opened [April 1900], and this can be explained by the custom that when an archbishop translated a saint's bones, he took one away with him.

1914 – February.   Much to the amazement of coastal villagers, who remember the shipwrecks of their childhood, the Rotterdam steamer *Dorothea* has had a miraculous escape from the grip of the Chesil Beach. She was washed ashore, off Langton Herring, in the middle of the month [14 February], broadsides and high and dry, but her iron hull withstood the experience. Dozens of spectators came along the beach from Portland, expecting to witness her imminent demise, but it is understood that she has since been refloated on a high tide and towed to sea and safety.

1914 – August. During that period of terrible anxiety, when war or peace were hanging in the balance, the uneventful life of Bridport went on, summer holidaymakers came to West Bay as usual, and there seemed no such hateful thing as war to mar and destroy the happiness which God intended for His creatures. But when the declaration of war was made known from the Bridport News office, all was changed. [War against Germany being announced to the House of Commons by Sir Edward Grey, the Secretary of State for Foreign Affairs, on 4 August 1914.] Hundreds of people daily besieged the offices for the latest news, and all became bustle and excitement, for there was scarcely a fighting ship on the sea without a Bridport man in her crew, many men from the town were serving in the Army, and time-expired men had passed into the Reserve.

1914 Colonel T. A. Colfox of Coneygar, Bridport, undertook the erection of a beacon on the East Cliff at West Bay, Captain Pass built up one on Thorncombe Beacon, another was at Abbotsbury, and so on east and west on the line. At that time it was considered possible that a German raiding party might land on our coast and their first move would be to cut the telegraph and telephone wires. In such an event there would have been no means of giving prompt notice to Portland but by those beacon fires.

1914 The War Office has commandeered the best horses in the county. In this, as in everything else, nothing matters but to win the war, and any trade inconvenience caused by the heavy drafts of horses from the neighbourhood is cheerfully borne in a spirit of patriotism. The Great Western Railway Company has but two dray horses left to do all the carting from the station yard at Bridport. Nearly all the brewery horses were taken, and farmers, carters and tradespeople generally were equally affected.

1915 – 1 January. HMS *Formidable*, sailing last in line with the Fifth Battle Squadron from Portland Harbour, was the first naval casualty of the new year, being torpedoed today, Friday, at 02.20 hours in Lyme Bay, off Lyme Regis, by a German submarine. Her position was 20 miles east of Start Point. An orderly evacuation was carried out for two hours, as the battleship appeared to be stable, but at 04.39 she slipped under quite suddenly. Deteriorating weather had hampered the rescue operation. Of the crew of 780, only 233 were saved, some in their own cutter which has taken 20 hours to reach the shore at Lyme Regis [where six are buried]. The Brixham trawler *Provident* carried out heroic rescues, as did the escort cruisers HMS *Topaze* and *Diamond*, which together brought a total of 80 survivors into Portland. U-boat UB-24 was responsible, with two torpedoes from close range, and in the process only narrowly survived – having grazed the heaving keel of the 15,000-ton warship. The ship's dog, an old terrier named Bruce, was also lost; he was last seen standing on duty beside his master, Captain Loxley, on the bridge. Rev. G. Brooke Robinson, formerly curate of Burton Bradstock and a prominent member of West Bay Swimming Club, was chaplain on board, and also went down with the ship. One of the ship's cutters, after being buffeted about in the gale for 20 hours, grounded on the beach in front of the Marine Parade, Lyme Regis, at about 22.45 this Friday night. It was one of only two boats that got away from the wreck, the other being picked up by Captain Pillar's Brixham trawler, which he put about at the peril of his own life, in one of the worst south-east gales of recent years.

1915 – January. Mr W. S. Edwards of The Gables at Bridport, the principal of net manufacturers Messrs. W. Edwards and Son, has been summoned to London for a conference with Mr Winston Churchill, the First Lord of the Admiralty, and Sir John Fisher, the First Sea Lord. Mr Churchill said that the only thing that could possibly defeat the British Navy was the submarine, and with the loss of the Navy there would be the probability of our losing the war. He explained that a naval officer had thought of using steel-wire nets for catching submarines in precisely the same way as nets were used for catching herrings, the only difference being the use of steel-wire cable instead of cotton thread. A specification is being drawn up for an Indicator (Anti-Submarine) Net.

1915 – 5 February. Today, Friday, is the last parade of the "Howe" Battalion, 2nd Royal Naval Brigade, of the Royal Naval Division, who arrived in Bridport in January for an intensive course of training. Commanded by Lieutenant-Colonel C. G. Collins, they distinguished themselves during the hurried retreat from Antwerp [October 1914], marching 31 miles during one night, to escape an encircling movement. There are close-on 1,000 fine, smart young fellows. They are digging elaborate entrenchments on Eype Down, skilfully laid out from five to six feet deep, in zig-zag formation. Whole days are spent in the trenches, exactly as in the fighting line, with cooking done under service conditions, and no man showing himself as snipers represent the enemy. On Sundays the trenches are visited by crowds of town and country people. The men are looking forward to renewing "auld acquaintance" with the town where they spent such pleasant days in their training. [Alas, few of them lived to gratify this desire, as they were bound for the Dardanelles, where nearly all were killed in the fighting at Gallipoli.]

1915 There is no longer freedom of movement as we have known it, for under the National Registration Act we are all now registered – name, occupation, and postal address – and supposed to carry the certificate with us when away from home, for presentation whenever it might be demanded.

1915 The French Impressionist painter Lucien Pissarro [born 1863], son of Camille Pissarro, has retreated from his nation at war to the peace of a Dorset country cottage at Fishpond Bottom, on the southern slopes of Lambert's Castle Hill. His summertime visitors included James Bolivar Manson of the Tate Gallery [then an assistant, rising to become its director in 1930]. They have become close friends and take every opportunity for a stroll into the surrounding countryside to paint together.

1915 – 31 December.   The extension to the Bridport railway, from the town to West Bay, has closed to passenger traffic for the duration of the hostilities.

1916   Steel-wire submarine nets, manufactured in Bridport by Messrs. W. Edwards and Son, are said to be accounting for an increasing number of enemy U-boats. Specially-designed motor launches, based for a time at West Bay, also play havoc amongst them. Airships from Powerstock, floating gracefully over the English Channel, can locate a submarine lurking in the water below, and swoop down to attack with bombs.

1916   Lyme Regis, on the other hand, has become a laughing stock for its spate of absurd U-boat alarms. One, which was actually reported to Scotland Yard, was that a German submarine base had been established in Pinhay Bay, on the ground that a man was found unconscious on the rocks one day, who, when he came round, made the statement that while standing looking toward the land someone came up from behind and knocked him on the head. A German sailor, from under the sea, became the popular explanation. Similarly, an elderly lady visitor, seeing a man around the same rocks each day, assumed he was sending wireless messages to U-boats; he was found to be picking limpets. Another man was accused of taking money for supplying petrol to German agents. Closer observation revealed it to be Mr Curtis, the town's best-known fossil hunter, selling his wares.

1917   A new Zero Airship, on an anti-submarine patrol from Mullion, Cornwall, turned inland towards the Admiralty Airship Station at Powerstock. It came too low after passing over Bridport and clipped treetops at Loders, coming down on a grassy slope above the railway line. Bombs were safely jettisoned and the pilot, John Owner, and his crew suffered only minor bruising.

1917   There is no such thing as wartime unemployment in Bridport and district. The town's netting works and their army of outworkers have produced hemp lanyards for the Army and Navy. White lanyards for sailors to wear around their necks and plaited and twisted shoulder lanyards are being delivered in millions, representing something like 300 tons in weight. Likewise tent-lines and twines of all descriptions. The Royal Navy's requirements include fishing seine nets, in large quantities, so that warships can catch fresh fish at sea. The Air Board is ordering balloon and aeroplane cordage, with one firm maintaining a continuous supply of six tons per week. This year the idea of camouflage netting has been widely adopted, not only for hiding away war material and gun emplacements, and so on, in France, but for generally disguising the movements of troops. This netting is being made in Bridport in huge quantities, both by machine and by hand, so much so that because of the big demand for women workers on the land as an alternative form of National Service, the War Office has instructed the manufacturers to issue the copy of a notice to all outworkers and braiders in the district. It is hoped to reassure them that in braiding these particular nets they are making their highest possible contribution to the war effort. Even such mundane products as potato nets and pea nets have a military application, being used by our troops for boiling these vegetables.

1917 – 28 June.   The French steamship *Marguerite* has been torpedoed and sunk by a German submarine, off Lyme Regis.

1917 – 20 July.   Two British steamships have been torpedoed and sunk today by German U-boats in Lyme Bay. They are the *L. H. Carl* and the *Salsette*, with the latter being last seen on the horizon off Lyme Regis.

1917 – 21 September.   *Radius*, a Danish steamship, has been sunk by a torpedo in Lyme Bay.

1917 – 23 September.   A British dredger, the *St. Dunstan*, has been torpedoed and sunk in Lyme Bay.

1917 – November.   With her headquarters at South Street in Bridport, Mrs C. F. S. Sanctuary of Mangerton has organised the Bridport War Hospital Supply Department. Her brother, Captain John Collings Taswell Glossop, was in command of the Australian cruiser *Sydney* when she sank the German raider *Emden* in the Indian Ocean [9 November 1914].

1918 – 18 March.   A 6,000-ton steamship, the *Baygitano*, has been torpedoed by a German U-boat just two miles off Lyme Regis. She began sinking immediately, as the local lifeboat *Thomas Masterman Hardy* was launched, and boats from the harbour also came to her aid. Conditions were calm as the captain and four men were taken off by the lifeboat, and the remainder of the crew by other vessels. Three had been killed in the explosion, ["The Wreck", as *Baygitano* is now known, has become a notable fishing ground.]

1918   A maid servant at Bridport put her name and address inside one of the pairs of socks she knitted for men at the Front. It came with bundles for the battery commanded by Major [later Sir] Philip Colfox [1888-1966]. The soldier who got them wrote to her full of gratitude, and from this a correspondence grew up. The first time he got leave he came on to Bridport, proposed to the girl, was accepted, and they were some time afterwards married, with a bright and happy prospect in front of them.

1918 – 28 June.   Captain Julian Royds Gribble [1897-1918] of Kingston Russell, fighting with the Royal Warwicks, has been gazetted for the Victoria Cross. [He died of his wounds.]

1918 Commander Victor Crutchley [1893-1986] of Mappercombe Manor, Nettlecombe, near Powerstock, has been awarded the Victoria Cross for his heroic second – and successful – attempt at blocking Ostend Harbour. The valiant first occasion was on 22-23 April 1918 when he was aboard HMS *Brilliant*. For that action the Jutland veteran was awarded the Distinguished Service Cross. Then he returned to Ostend in the repeat operation of 9-10 May aboard the block-ship HMS *Vindictive*, stuffed with explosives, and nearly became part of her sacrifice. Again he narrowly escaped with his life and this time the reward was not only Britain's highest honour but the French Croix de Guerre as well. [Admiral Sir Victor Crutchley, as he became, remained at sea between the wars and commanded the 30,600-ton battleship HMS *Warspite* from 1937 to 1940. After a spell ashore as the Commodore at Devonport he returned to the water to command the Australian Naval Squadron, 1942-44. He was then Flag Officer Gibraltar until retirement in 1947. There followed four decades as the white-bearded village patriarch. He is buried in Powerstock churchyard, beneath a striking wooden cross redolent of another age. It is surmounted with the "For Valour" insignia of the Victoria Cross.]

1918 – 11 November. The first news of the Armistice came by wireless to the Royal Naval Airship Station at Powerstock, at 6.30 in the morning, straight from Paris, stating that hostilities will cease at eleven o'clock. The message was telephoned to the Mayor of Bridport, who received it at eight o'clock. This had been hourly expected, and the streets of the town were already thronged when the new Mayor, Councillor E. S. Reynolds, announced the news. It was received by the people with an outburst of cheering, and the day was made a holiday. The bells of St Mary rang out joyous peals and the town clock, which had been silent throughout the war, struck again at the hour of eleven, marking the official time for cessation of hostilities.

1919 – March. Bridport responded magnificently to the national appeal for eggs, for nursing casualties of the fighting forces during the Great War, over a four-year period from March 1915. These were taken to the receiving station at the Town Hall, from where 1,636 eggs were dispatched to Military Hospitals at Exeter, and a grand total of 62,793 went to Headquarters for the Base Hospitals in France and other hospitals at home. [Representing a donation worth £1,700, given that the top price for eggs reached 6s. 6d. a dozen in 1918.]

1919 – 7 July. The Bridport holiday line, the extension railway from the town to its seaside resort of West Bay, today re-opened to passenger traffic after having been closed during the Great War.

1920   A stone seat has been erected on the seaward side of the Hardy Monument as a memorial to Major William Digby Oswald who was killed on the Somme, at the age of 36 [16 July 1916], by the shell-band from a British gun which fired prematurely. A "soldier's soldier", Oswald had seen action behind enemy lines and was a veteran of the Boer War, Natal rebellion, and Zulu rising. He was buried on the Somme, at Dives Copse near Bray, but his comrades decided upon an English memorial, overlooking the Weymouth countryside where he had met his wife, Catherine Yardley.

1924 – 10 January.   HM Submarine *L24* was today rammed by the battle-cruiser HMS *Resolution* and sank with all hands. The collision occurred in Lyme Bay, to the west of Portland Bill. The captain, Lieutenant-Commander Paul L. Eddis, drowned with his 42 officers and men.

1926 – 5 December.   A combination of slipping clay and an angry sea has ripped out a length of Lyme's promenade at Marine Parade.

1928   Royal doctor Sir Maurice Abbot-Anderson [1861-1938] has retired to Madeira Cottage, Lyme Regis. He founded Flora's

League to campaign for the conservation of wild flowers. This work is being actively supported by Lady Muriel Abbot-Anderson [1888-1973].

1928   Adela Curtis [1864-1960], the author of *The New Mysticism* [1907], has established a celibate and contemplative vegetarian Christian commune for women, to work the land around the newly-built St Bride's Farm, Burton Bradstock. She has lectured and written of her experiences with a similar community, the Order of Silence, which she founded at Coldash, Berkshire, in 1912.

1930 – 12 January.   A storm-lashed French ketch, the *Reine des Cieux*, has been washed ashore at Eype, a mile from West Bay. Her crew of three were successfully taken off in Lyme Bay by the Torbay lifeboat.

1930 – 22 September.   Passenger trains to West Bay ceased with today's services, the extension line from Bridport town to the coast having failed to coincide with development of a strong hotel trade, though the line is to be kept open for goods working.

1932 – 13 October.   The decision has been taken to close the Lyme Regis lifeboat station. Coverage in Lyme Bay will be provided by a new motor-powered lifeboat from Exmouth.

1934 – 23 December.   "Sink the *Emden*" hero Vice-Admiral John Collings Taswell Glossop [1871-1934] died today in Dorset. He went from a naval education into the service, as a midshipman [1887] and sailed to Polynesia with the *Calliope* [1889] and became Lieutenant of the *Royalist*, intervening during the Samoan troubles [1899]. He reached the rank of captain shortly before the Great War and was commander of the Australian cruiser HMS *Sydney* at the destruction of the German raider *Emden*, following a lengthy search, off Direction Island in the Cocos Keeling group in the Indian Ocean [9 November 1914]. Promoted Rear Admiral [1922], he retired Vice-Admiral [1926], returning to Britain and living at Little Wych, Burton Road, Bridport. His honours included Companion of the Bath, Officer of the Legion of Honour, and from Japan the Order of the Rising Sun (3rd class).

1937 – January. At the end of the month the worst snowstorm for many years raged across west Dorset, leaving huge drifts between Bridport and Dorchester. Cars were stranded along the main road and a hundred people spent the night at the Askers Road House on the crest of the downs.

1937 Fred Welch, Bridport's town crier since 1925, has won the National Town Criers Competition.

1937 The Royal Air Force has opened a Marine Craft Unit at Lyme Regis, using launches for air-sea rescue and stand-by duties in connection with bombing and experimental flights planned over Lyme Bay and the Chesil Beach.

1938 The St Bride's Christian Contemplatives' Community at Burton Bradstock, which was founded by the mystic writer Adela Curtis in 1928, has been provided with a large chapel. The community's rules and constitution were enshrined in a trust deed, signed on 21 December, which precludes papists and Christian Scientists from the commune and also bans the installation of water closets, because sewerage is at the basis of their organic methods of growing produce. Piped water is also prohibited, as are electricity and the "fossil" fuels. There are seven periods of prayer each day, beginning at 5 am. Local people call the members of the community the "White Ladies" because of their cream veils and robes.

1938 The National Trust has acquired the freehold of the Hardy Monument, commemorating Vice-Admiral Sir Thomas

Hardy of "Kiss me, Hardy" fame, having held a lease on the 72-feet tower for many years [see entry for 1901]. The Trust has also purchased three-quarters of an acre of the surrounding Black Down hilltop between Portesham and Martinstown. Colonel Sir Robert Williams has provided a fund for maintenance.

1939 – August. Lyme Regis Bombing Range, covering 16 square miles of sea, has been designated by the Air Ministry for daylight use. An initial limit of 120-lb has been imposed on live bombs that can be dropped.

1939 – 5 September. Two days into the new war, in today's K Destroyer Flotilla News, the daily newspaper of the 5th Destroyer Flotilla, Bob Knight reports to the crew of HMS *Kelly* on the fishy sequel resulting from anti-submarine depth charges that yesterday claimed a U-boat off Bridport. "That's war – that was; but we must not lead ourselves to believe that some of the catch will always appear on the breakfast table. The presence of mind of Posty in producing a gaff to lift the whales inboard while the ship had stopped to obtain a sample of the oil on the sea is much to be admired. We all hope that the *Kelly's* and *Acheron's* efforts [another destroyer] did away with one of the pests that sank, without warning, the liner *Athenia* on Sunday night [3 September, off Ireland] – and, of course, we hope that the lucky messes in the *Kelly* enjoyed their breakfast. There is plenty of corroborative evidence to show that there were two U-boats here yesterday, one in Weymouth Bay and one in West Bay. The periscope of the former was seen from the signal bridge of the *Resolution* and the M.A.S.B. and the tracks of two torpedoes fired at the *Kelly*. They missed us by 30 or 40 yards, so certainly we were lucky. To be missed by one submarine and bag another [later, in Lyme Bay] all in the first day [at sea, from Portland] is good going."

1939 – Christmas. News of the exciting naval action at the Battle of the River Plate has been marred for Powerstock villagers by the death of seaman Arthur Samuel Riglar [killed 13 December 1939]. He was serving aboard HMS *Exeter* which was severely damaged in the action which trapped the German pocket-battleship *Graf Spee*.

1940 – 12 April.   A laurel wreath hangs on the door of the Hardy Monument, the memorial to Nelson's flag captain on the hills above Portesham – the village known to Thomas Hardy as "Possum" – in memory of the men of the Royal Navy who lost their lives two days ago in Narvik fjord, Norway. A card reads: "To the unfading memory of Captain Warburton-Lee, RN, HMS *Hardy*, and the gallant men who died at Narvik. Nelson's Hardy and Hardy's Possum salute you."

1940 – 8 June.   Lieutenant-Commander   Charles   John Thompson Stephens was lost this afternoon in the sinking of the aircraft-carrier *Glorious*, off Narvik, by gunfire from the German battlecruisers *Scharnhorst* and *Gneisenau*. He was aged 35. Commander Thompson was the son of Major John August Stephens of Evershot, who served in the Royal Field Artillery and died in 1925, after a prolonged illness that resulted from injuries suffered in the Great War.

1940 – June.   Sometimes pub names have to move with events. Such was Bridport's King of Prussia, at 52 East Street, which became the King of Belgium when he was the nation's darling for standing up to the Kaiser in 1915. Now, however, he has capitulated to the next wave of invading Germans. This time Palmer's Brewery are choosing a hero who cannot be deposed – they have decided that Lord Nelson has stood the test of time.

1940 – July.   Thirty-two underground hideouts have been established secretly by the Royal Engineers in woods and commons scattered through the Dorset countryside to conceal the weapons, explosives and food necessary for Auxiliary Units of British Resistance to operate behind German lines in the event of an invasion.

1940 – 15 August. Twenty-seven-year-old Squadron Leader Terence Lovell-Gregg of 87 Squadron, from RAF Exeter, failed in a desperate attempt to make a crash landing in The Fleet lagoon late this afternoon. The Hurricane came in blazing over the sea but was brought into a controlled descent for a forced landing. *P3215* then clipped a tree beside Abbotsbury Swannery and its wounded pilot fell to his death. Flying Officer Roland Prosper Beamont, one of the Exeter pilots, returned with the story of how Lovell-Gregg had led his squadron into the midst of a mass of German aircraft at 18,000 feet over the English Channel: "We saw the 'Beehive' almost straight ahead at the same height, and with his Hurricanes, Lovell-Gregg flew straight at the centre of the formation without hesitation or deviation in any way." One hundred and twenty enemy aircraft were heading towards Portland. Lovell-Gregg was a quiet pre-war professional, from Marlborough in New Zealand, who had taught many of the emergent generation of flyers. His courage was never in any doubt, though he had led his squadron for only a month, since 12 July. The pilots knew him as "Shovel". There were only four of them with him when they scrambled at 16.00 hours today. Five Hurricanes were all the air-worthy machines that 87 Squadron could muster. Undaunted by the adverse odds of fifteen-to-one that loomed in front, Lovell-Gregg asked the impossible of his men: "Come on chaps, let's surround them!"

1940 – August. Writing in *The Two Edged Sword*, Adela Curtis, leader of the Christian Contemplatives' Community at St Bride's Farm, Burton Bradstock, advises on methods of furthering the war effort through positive prayer: "We are to summon each enemy leader by name. For cumulative effect the message should be spoken three times – Adolf Hitler! Adolf Hitler! Adolf Hitler! Hear the Truth!"

1940 – 7 September. The German invasion appears to have started. Reports have been received of a seven-mile convoy heading towards the Dorset coast and there is a general flap on that Operation Sealion is taking place and Field-Marshal Fedor von Bock is on his way with the victors of Poland, the Wehrmacht's Army Group B. The fuel tanks are to be fired to set the beaches ablaze and an aircraft from Gosport is dropping incendiaries to start them off. Troops at Bournemouth have manned the cliffs and keep emphasising that this is not an exercise.

1940 – 7 September 20.07 hours. A national alert has been issued by the War Office: "Condition Cromwell". An invasion is regarded as imminent and probable within 12 hours. [Nothing happened! Despite that, invasion fears reached fever-pitch, though not without reason, for aerial reconnaissances were showing concentrations of ships and barges from Brest to Calais.]

1940 – 15 September. 14.30 hours. The tall 1873-built tower of Cattistock parish church has been gutted by fire, destroying its famous carillon of 35 bells. The village will miss the tunes. Officially the cause is not known, but locally it has been blamed on a cigarette discarded by a member of the Home Guard who was in the tower for fire-watching.

1940 – 8 October. Pilot Officer Harold John Akroyd of 152 Squadron from RAF Warmwell has died at the Dorset County Hospital, Dorchester, from burns received yesterday when his crippled Spitfire, N3039, burst into flames on crashing at Shatcombe Farm, Wynford Eagle. It had been crippled by enemy fire in the dog-fights over west Dorset. He was aged 27, and will be buried in the RAF plot at Warmwell churchyard.

1940 – 7 October.   A Junkers Ju.88 bomber (9K+SN), heading for the Westland Aircraft Factory at Yeovil, was brought down at 16.20 hours on Tappers Hill, above the hamlet of Up Sydling, near Sydling St. Nicholas. The kill has been claimed jointly by Sergeant Pilot Edmund Shepperd of 152 Squadron from Warmwell and Flying Officer Bob Doe in a Hurricane of 238 Squadron from RAF Chilbolton. All four members of the German crew baled out successfully and were taken prisoners of war, after being rounded up by shotgun, following which the farm labourers performed a victory dance around the wreckage. The crewmen were Oberfeldwebel Sigurd Hey, Leutnant Friedrich Bein, Oberfeldwebel Christian Koenig, and Oberfeldwebel Josef Troll. The bomber belonged to the 5th Staffel of II Gruppe Kamfgruppe 51.

1940 – 7 October.   Messerchmitt Bf.110C (3U+JP) of the 6th Staffel of Zerstorergeschwader 26, which had been defending the bombers en route to the Westland Aircraft Company works at Yeovil, has crashed at Brickhills Field, near Kingston Russell House. Crewmen Obergefreiter Herbert Schilling and Oberfeldwebel Karl Herzog were killed on impact. [Further human remains were removed, together with wreckage and identification papers, during an excavation carried out by Andy Saunders in 1976. The flyers' graves are in the German War Cemetery at Cannock Chase. A propeller from the crash is displayed in the offices of Dorset Country Magazine.]

1940 – 14 October.   The British armed trawler HMT *Lord Stamp* has sunk after striking a mine in Lyme Bay.

1940 – 17 October.   The Royal Navy's losses of armed trawlers to the German minefield off west Dorset continued today when HMT *Kingston Cairngorm* blew-up off Portland Bill.

1940 – 6 November.   In the early morning a Heinkel He.111 of Kampfgruppe 100, the elite two per cent of German bombers operating from Vannes, Brittany, and acting as pathfinders for the attacking formations, suffered a compass failure. It was confused by the British masking of German radio beacons into thinking it was back over France when in fact it was running out of fuel above Dorset. The pilot landed on the shingle beach at West Bay, Bridport, and three out of the four crew survived – though they soon had their illusions shattered regarding France and found themselves in captivity. Soldiers guarded the aircraft, which carried the identification code "6N", and had some difference of opinion with a naval detachment that came to drag the plane up the beach. The soldiers followed orders not to let anyone touch the bomber and it was engulfed by the incoming tide. The aircraft has three vertical aerials and related radio equipment. This apparatus is to be salvaged for inspection by Air Ministry boffins.

1940 – 21 November.   Scientists   at   the   Royal   Aircraft Establishment, Farnborough, have reassembled radio beam-flying equipment removed from the Heinkel He.111 bomber of the Luftwaffe's pathfinding Kampfgruppe 100 which crash-landed at West Bay on 6 November. The aircraft had three vertical aerials and an intact X-Gerat radio receiver, also known as Wotan I, which is used for precision bombing by enabling the aircraft to follow a radio direction beam emanating from the Cherbourg peninsula. What has surprised the Air Ministry experts is that the apparatus is tuned to 2000 cycles per second (approximating to the "C" which is two octaves above standard-pitch middle "C"), whereas British jamming countermeasures   had   assumed   a   note   of   1500   cycles (approximating to the "G" below this upper "C"). They are less than pleased that the vital equipment was corroded and full of sand, this avoidable damage to the delicate light-alloy components being due to the crass folly of the Dorset soldiers who prevented sailors from pulling the aircraft up the beach to safety. It became awash with the rising tide. Particular anger has been expressed that the secret could have been cracked in time to foil the Coventry raid, which took place a week ago: "Someone in Dorset should be shot!"

1941 – 27 March. Wing Commander Edward Collis de Virac Lart [1902-41] of Lyme Regis, whose flying career began in the 1920s with 60 (Bombing) Squadron in India, is missing, presumed dead, on failing to return to his base.

1941 An RAF Blenheim, returning from Bomber Command's raid on the port of Brest, crashed last night at Frampton, five miles north-west of Dorchester. The three crewmen, Sergeants P. I. Burrows, G. B. H. Birdsell and H. R. Perry, were killed instantaneously as the aeroplane exploded on hitting the ground. T2439 belonged to 101 Squadron and had taken off from RAF West Raynham, Norfolk, at 19.15 hours. She crashed while trying to chart a course to RAF Boscombe Down which is 45 miles to the north-east.

1941 – 10 May. The Spitfire appeal in west Dorset, which raised nearly £6,000, has paid for Spitfire R7062 which was today handed over to 308 Squadron. It is being named "The Brit" after Bridport's river. [The fighter was transferred to 403 Squadron, on 28 May 1941, and later to a training unit near Chester. It was lost in a flying accident on 21 December 1941.]

1941 – June. Lyme Regis has contributed no less than £69,222 "towards sending another ship to fight in His Majesty's Navy for the freedom of mankind from the Nazi thrall". This is £25.10s. per head from the 2,700 inhabitants. Champion town crier Walter Abbott made the announcement of "this Empire's determination to guard our rightful place on the good Earth." [The town's special warship would be the Bangor-class minesweeper HMS *Lyme Regis*, a 650-ton vessel launched from Alexander Stephens and Sons yards on the Clyde, 19 March 1942.]

1941 – 10 December. Seaman John Henry Brabant from Powerstock was among those killed when Japanese aircraft sank the battlecruiser HMS *Repulse* in the Indian Ocean.

1941 – 17 December.   When their starboard engine failed last night, five crewmen of Wellington X9785 baled out over Chilfrome, eight miles north-west of Dorchester. The pilot, Sergeant Vezina, successfully brought his crippled bomber to a crash-landing at Holm Farm, above West Milton, near Powerstock. The Wellington, belonging to 218 Squadron, had taken off from RAF Marham, Norfolk, at 18.40 hours to attack the German capital ships in the French Atlantic port of Brest.

1942 – 14 May.   The occupants of an RAF coastal radar station at Cain's Folly, on the cliffs east of Charmouth, had a shock when the ground literally opened up beneath them. A landslip carried away concrete buildings and has deposited them on the tumbled undercliff some 50 feet below.

1942 – 9 July.   This has been the Battle of Lyme Bay, carried out by the German 1st Schnellboot Flotilla (S48, S50, S63, S67, S70, S104, S109) against Allied Coast Convoy E/P 91. 12,192-tons of shipping has gone down; the tanker *SS Pomella* and four freighters. One of the British escorts has also been lost, an armed trawler, HMT *Manor*.

1942 – 4 December.   Barnes Neville Wallis, the assistant chief designer at the aviation section of Vickers-Armstrongs Limited, flew today from their Weybridge works to the Chesil Beach Bombing Range. He was in Wellington BJ895/G, an aeroplane he designed, and acted as the bomb aimer when the pilot, Captain J. "Mutt" Summers, came in low over the flat waters of The Fleet lagoon which lies between the offshore pebble bank and the inshore coast of Langton Herring and Abbotsbury. Captain R. C. Handasyde acted as the observer. Two steel spheres were dropped, with the hope that they might bounce along the surface of the water, but both burst upon impact. Neither carried explosives.

1942 – 15 December.   Wellington BJ895/G put down at Warmwell Aerodrome en route for further testings of the bouncing-bomb designed by scientist Barnes Wallis of Vickers-Armstrongs. As with their first test, on 4 December, both drops failed. It is decided to try again after Christmas.

1943 – 9 January. Two more steel spheres were dropped today by Wellington BJ895/G, from the Vickers-Armstrongs Weybridge works, on the Chesil Beach Bombing Range. The tests were once again a failure. The aim of aircraft designer Barnes Wallis is to devise a bomb that can bounce across the water and have a dam-breaking capability. So far, of the six dummy bombs that have been dropped, five have fragmented on touching The Fleet lagoon and the other was incorrectly released and hit the land.

1943 – 10 January. Vickers-Armstrongs scientist Barnes Wallis last night carried out modifications to one of his prototype bouncing-bombs at Warmwell Aerodrome. Wellington BJ895/G lifted off with it today for another low-level drop over The Fleet lagoon at Chesil Beach Bombing Range. The boffin and his crew are jubilant! For the first time their bomb, which had been strengthened, skimmed the surface of the water. It spun for 50 feet and then shattered – but the principle had been proved.

1943 – 23 January. Wellington BJ895/G today dropped a wooden version of the bouncing-bomb devised by Vickers-Armstrongs designer Barnes Wallis. It achieved thirteen bounces on the inshore lagoon of The Fleet to the east of Langton Hive Point, Langton Herring, on the RAF's Chesil Beach Bombing Range.

1943 – 24 January. Twenty bounces were recorded this morning by scientist Barnes Wallis as his revolutionary bomb zipped across The Fleet lagoon at Langton Herring. Once again it had been dropped from Wellington bomber BJ895/G which then flew back to Warmwell Aerodrome. The team from the Vickers-

Armstrongs Weybridge works then prepared a boom across the shallow waters. This is intended to simulate the wall of a dam. The evening saw another successful trial when the Wellington returned to the Chesil Beach Bombing Range. It again turned over the sea and came in across the lake-like waters of The Fleet. The bomb was dropped, and bounced, and proceeded to jump the boom.

1943 – 5 February.   The trials of wooden prototypes of Barnes Wallis's bouncing-bomb resumed on The Fleet today. They were dropped from Wellington BJ895/G, coming from Weybridge and operating for the day out of Warmwell Aerodrome. The bomber is now making faster approach runs. It swept in across the Chesil Beach Bombing Range at 300 miles per hour and succeeded in sending bombs jumping across the sheltered and wave-less inshore water for distances around 4,000 feet.

1943 – 28 February.   In the past four days the 5th Schnellboot Flotilla has been harrying a Channel convoy in Lyme Bay and onwards between Portland and the Isle of Wight. Two of the escorts protecting Convoy CHA 172 the armed trawlers HMT *Harstad* and HMT *Lord Hailsham* have been sunk. The freighter *Moldavia* (4,858 tons) has also gone down, together with a new 658-ton tank landing craft, *LCT381*.

1943 – February.   A Dornier Do.17 bomber, shot down at night over South Buckham Farm, Beaminster, has been claimed by Wing Commander Rupert Clerke, flying a Beaufighter of 125 (Newfoundland) Squadron from RAF Fairwood Common, Glamorgan.

1943 – 9 March.   Carrying fully-weighted steel versions of the prototype bouncing-bomb devised for dam-busting operations by designer Barnes Wallis of Vickers-Armstrongs, Wellington BJ895/G returned yesterday to Warmwell Aerodrome and the Chesil Beach Bombing Range for an extended series of trial runs over The Fleet lagoon. The dummy bombs are skimming the water with the precision that suggests their use as an effective weapon is now feasible. These trials concluded this evening. Locally, there have been complaints that the Wellington's approach flight, at 300 miles per hour over the West Fleet towards Langton Hive Point, and the uninhabited Herbury peninsula, has been upsetting nest-building at the famous Abbotsbury Swannery. [The next set of tests, to determine the handling behaviour of the bomb on choppier water, would take place off Reculver, Kent.]

1943 – 17 May.   The earliest versions of the bouncing bombs that were dropped last night by Lancasters of 617 Squadron, to breach the Mohne and Eder dams in the Ruhr, were tested in Dorset. Prototypes of the weapon had been developed on a freelance basis by Barnes Wallis of Vickers-Armstrongs, working outside the official Ministry of Aircraft Production's armament programme. They were carried by a Wellington and dropped from 60 feet on to the flat waters of The Fleet lagoon, near Langton Herring. This part of the Chesil Beach Bombing Range was used to ascertain that the bombs worked in principle, skimming across the water like a well-thrown stone, though the actual practice runs for Operation Chastise were carried out by the Lancasters over the Elan valley reservoir in the mountains of mid-Wales. [Air Marshal Arthur Harris, Commander-in-Chief Bomber Command, recalled that he "rang up Washington, where Churchill and Portal were at the time, and there was some little difficulty. When I did get through I was intercepted and asked for an assurance that the person I was calling was reliable. I don't know whether she was persuaded that Winston Churchill came into that category, but I got through to Portal in the end and told him that the two dams had gone." Eight of the 19 Lancasters failed to return. The main aim had been to cause a shortage for industrial purposes in the Ruhr, rather than sweeping everything away in a flood, which is how we tend to remember the exploit. Not that there were many happy farmers in Kassel when 330 million tons of water spread across their fields. Several hundred Russian prisoners-of-war were among the 1,294 people who drowned.]

1943 – 31 August.   The Daily Telegraph reports that a Lyme Regis hotelier received a stamped addressed postcard from an anxious prospective visitor asking for "the date of the last enemy attack on your town". The manager sent the card back with the date – "1685".

1943 – December.   Perhaps the kindest sequel to a war story in the past few months has been that of RAF Sergeant Pilot Ronald Foss, from Bridport, who was on a Coastal Command flight over the Bay of Biscay. The first person to know he was missing happened to be his wife, whom he married in April 1942, as she was serving in the operations room of the same air station. Ronald, in fact, was still alive, and would be picked up from the sea a week later with enough experiences of war to fill a book. [Or, rather, three of them. The titles were *In the Drink*, *Three of us Live*, and *Famous War Stories*.]

1944 – 16 April.   Though expected to gather in Portland and Weymouth for Operation Overlord, British invasion Force G has been relocated eastwards to the harbours and inlets of the Solent and Southampton Water. Instead the Dorset ports are being allocated to United States Force O. They are destined for what is designated as Omaha Beach and the British troops are to land in the next sector to the east, codenamed Gold Beach. Today Captain J. J. McGlynn of the United States Navy takes up his post as Commanding Officer United States Navy Advanced Amphibious Base Portland and Weymouth. This includes the three hards at Portland and HMS *Grasshopper*, the Royal Navy shore-base at Weymouth, plus ancillary facilities. Captain McGlynn will be responsible for the embarkation of V Corps of the First United States Army which comprises the 1st US Infantry division, 2nd US Infantry Division, 2nd US Armored Division, and two Ranger battalions. The "Fighting Firsts" or "Big Red One", as America's famous First Infantry Division is known, has its Divisional Headquarters at Langton House,

Langton Long Blandford. The Commanding General, Major-General Clarence R. Huebner, has at his command 34,142 men and 3,306 vehicles. It is estimated that there must now be a total of 80,000 American soldiers who are billeted in Dorset, from the chalets of Freshwater holiday camp on the coast at Burton Bradstock to Nissen huts in hazel coppices on Cranborne Chase.

1944 – 6 June.   Dorset's Americans are the heroes of "Bloody Omaha", the scene of the worst Allied casualties of the D-Day invasion. They are reported to have lost 3,000 lives on this "Decision Day" with their beach-head objectives eventually secured as dusk dropped on this longest day. [Total losses in the Battle of Normandy would be 37,000 Allied dead, and 58,000 German fatalities.]

1947 – 4 August.   Major A. B. Hartley of Southern Command announced yesterday that the 16th and 17th Bomb Disposal squads of the Royal Engineers had so far disposed of 9,000 anti-invasion mines along the coast eastwards from Weymouth. This includes a total of some 3,200 from a mile of shingle beach and clayey cliffs at Ringstead Bay. The operations have so far cost the lives of three officers and 22 other ranks. One officer has been blinded.

1947   Fred Welch of Bridport has again won the National Town Criers Championship. He took the title in 1937. [He also became the first town crier to appear on television, in the "Picture Page" programme with Phyllis Robins and Gillie Potter.]

1948   The film *All Over the Town* has been completed at Lyme Regis, which stars under the guise of Tormouth.

1948   Litton Cheney Friendly Society, which was founded in the Hungry Forties [in 1844] held its last club walk and church service on Whit Tuesday. For a century it has provided for the sick and destitute of the village. "Walking", as this annual club fete was known, was the major community occasion of the year. Everyone appeared in their best attire and marched behind a band and an embroidered banner seven feet high and eight feet wide. The new National Insurance scheme [which came into operation on 5 July] has put an end to the last of the village benevolent societies.

1950   Dorset pet shops are catering for the craze for golden hamsters, which has spread from London and threatens to displace rabbits from their cages. After all we now live in an age when we no longer have to eat our pets. These are not only tiny but scrupulously clean and wash with their paws like a cat. Great bulges around their necks are nothing to cause alarm, merely being surplus food which is stored in a pouch. This helped them survive in the Syrian desert and all are said to descend from a single pregnant female.

1950   Charlie Ford of Clayhanger Farm, south-east of Abbotsbury, who was known as the "Dorset Singing Minstrel" because of his repertoire of countless traditional folk songs, has been killed in a road accident. He was 54.

1950   Abbotsbury fisherman Jack Keech, a former gamekeeper and wartime commando, has caught and killed the basking-shark that was nicknamed Moby Dick and had broken numerous nets along this stretch of coast. The 15-feet carcass lies rotting on the shingle, perforated by knife-cuts inflicted by Keech and his crew. They netted the shark in shallow water and dragged it ashore.

1951   Sometimes in the winter gales the tide will break right over the "winter ridge" of the Chesil Beach at Burton Freshwater and come pouring across farmer Bunny Lenthall's water-meadows into Burton Bradstock village, flooding the road, halting all traffic, and swirling into the old low-lying cottages.

1952   On 14 September, after a fight over 18 months between the railway executive and the local authorities, the railway line from

Upwey to Abbotsbury closed to all traffic because of "the economic circumstances". Recently a film was shot in the West Country, under somewhat similar circumstances [The Titfield Thunderbolt], and in the story the closed line was purchased, re-opened, and privately operated. There's an idea for someone in Weymouth!

1952 A memorial to the war-dead of the 43rd (Wessex) Division was unveiled on a wooded ridge above Winyard's Gap, Chedington, on 20 September. It is a replica of the memorial on Hill 112 near Caen, Normandy, which the infantrymen stormed, and was unveiled by General Sir Ivor Thomas. [Similar memorials were erected on Castle Hill, Mere, and at Rough Tor, Cornwall, to give views spreading to all the counties from which this Territorial division recruited. It included battalions of the Dorsetshire Regiment.]

1953 On Coronation Day the Abbotsbury fishermen caught another shark. This was a thresher-shark, smaller and more dangerous than a basker. They put the shark on a lorry, and entered it for the carnival procession, with the notice, "You should have seen the one that got away"; and received second prize for their effort.

1955 – 19 July. The cloudburst over west Dorset deposited more rain, in the past 24 hours, than has ever been previously recorded in the British Isles. It remained quasi-stationary for several hours, falling intensely from about 14.30 hours yesterday to 19.00 hours, with the heaviest falls in the second half of this period. With a total of eleven inches at Martinstown, where N. I. Symonds's rain gauge at the Chantry was overflowing, it far exceeded that which caused the Lynton and Lynmouth floods [15 August 1952], though fortunately without fatalities as west of Dorchester the water dispersed into different catchment areas. Its epicentre was between Winterbourne Steepleton and the Hardy Monument, where in excess of twelve inches must have fallen, and deep gouges have been cut in the hillsides of Coryates Gap and Corton Hill. Eastwards, the tea garden was swept away from beside the Picnic Inn at Osmington Mills, being typical of damage that is physically impressive but unimportant. It is estimated that three-quarters of a million gallons fell per square mile, compared with half a million gallons per square mile on Exmoor, in the case of the Lynmouth disaster. It has been a fine, hot summer until this anticyclone arrived, bringing thunderstorms, with a surface temperature of 84 degrees Fahrenheit being recorded at Bridport. Such summertime deluges have led to a widespread belief that something is happening to our weather [popularly blamed on atomic weapons testing] but it is impossible, from the available data, to say why the amount of rainfall was so large on this occasion. Meteorologists, who are employed by the War Department, insist that such cloudbursts, although exceptional, are part of normal weather patterns.

1959 – 15 June.　The last two 45XX class 2-6-2 steam tank engines to work the Bridport branch railway, numbers 4507 and 4562, were today withdrawn to Weymouth motive-power depot. They have been replaced by diesel units.

1960　Adela Curtis, who was born in 1864, died on 17 September. Her memorial in the chapel which she built at the Christian Contemplatives' Charity, St Bride's Farm, Burton Bradstock, reads: "I have loved thee with an everlasting love." She had wished to be buried in the garden there but was cremated at Weymouth; which went against her beliefs in two ways as she disapproved of the use of gas and advocated that all natural wastes should be returned to the soil.

1962　The skull, it is thought, of the Duke of Monmouth, has been discovered under 10 Downing Street during an excavation by Ministry of Works archaeologist Michael Green, it was reported on 8 March. It was found in a container that had been hewn from a single piece of stone that was just long enough to hold it. Experts say that the head is of a man in his thirties executed at least 250 years ago, hit by a blunt axe on the forehead and by a mass of cuts on the back of the neck. The Duke's axing is known to have been bungled; he was struck many times. He had lodgings in Whitehall Palace, on the Treasury site, and the place where the skull was found may have been his garden. A further clue was that the skull had been exposed for a time, as would have been the custom. Although some remains of the Duke were found in Victorian times in the chapel of St Peter ad Vincula in the Tower of London these do not appear to have included the head. It may be safely presumed that the head would have been put on public display. Monmouth, the bastard son of Charles II, was beheaded at the age of 36, after his landing at Lyme Regis and defeat on the battlefield of Sedgemoor, in the abortive Western Rebellion against James II in 1685.

1962 – December.   All operational use has now ceased on the southern end of the Bridport railway, from the town to West Bay, with its closure to goods traffic.

1962 – 30 December.   The final Sunday of the year saw a blizzard which deposited a foot of snow all across Dorset. Much more is lying in drifts, says Chief Constable Arthur Hambleton who has requested the BBC to broadcast a message, advising motorists not to travel into Dorset because main roads are blocked. Over 100 cars are caught in a slithering queue on one of the many hills on the A35 between Bridport and Dorchester, at Askerswell, with Bridport police finding accommodation for 50 stranded travellers. Ninety-two people are also being put up at the Bull Hotel in East Street, where every available space is in use, such as bathrooms and the former Bridport Borough Council Social Club. "Wherever we can put up a bed, we have someone," said hotel director Mrs Elizabeth Forbes. To the north-east there are further problems, with the A37 being entirely blocked all the way from Stratton to Warden Hill, above Evershot.

1963 – 25 August. Two steam pannier-tank locomotives of the old Great Western Railway, numbers 7782 and 4689, hauled a special train from Bridport to West Bay to give the town's coastal railway its last rites. The excursion was chartered by the Southern Counties Touring Society. [The track would be lifted in 1965. Two decades later, West Bay Station was restored and a short section of rails re-laid, as a tourist attraction, at the end of the line.]

1964 – August. The RAF has closed its Marine Craft Unit at Lyme Regis.

1965 The Christian Contemplatives' Community at Burton Bradstock have handed over their chapel, house, and land to the Othona Community founded by ex-RAF padre Canon Norman Motley, at Bradwell in Essex, in 1946.

1966 The playwright Robert Cedric Sherriff [1896-1975], on leaving Downhouse Farm above Eype, has given its 176 acres to the National Trust. Southwards the land rises into the great coastal headland of Thorncombe Beacon, and in the other direction it links with the wild expanse of Eype Common, where the Trust holds grazing rights.

1967 – 8 June. A new lifeboat station has been built at Lyme Regis, on the shore at the Cobb, to house a fast inflatable inshore rescue vessel. Yesterday she carried out her first rescue, saving two from the stricken yacht *Wren*, and today four were taken off *Black Panther*, a speedboat. The formal inauguration ceremony to open the station is still two days' away.

1969 *The French Lieutenant's Woman*, by Lyme Regis novelist John Fowles [born 31 March 1926] is set in the town and on its adjoining Undercliff and has been nationally acclaimed as the most important Dorset book since the works of Thomas Hardy. John and Elizabeth Fowles lived at Underhill Farm, on the coast west of the town, but moved to Belmont House, overlooking the Cobb, after a landslip. [Where the book would be filmed, and on the Undercliff, starring Jeremy Irons and Meryl Streep.]

1969   Britain's most active landslip continues to move, from 477-feet on the cliffs west of Charmouth, down through the entire Black Ven undercliff, which has become a treacherous mudflow impossible to cross. It has overwhelmed the beach and slid 200 yards out to sea with a spit that projects across the Canary Ledges.

1960s   This decade, the Swinging Sixties, is judged to have been best summed up in *The Knack*, by playwright Anne Jellicoe [born 1927]. From her home at Colway Manor, Colway Lane, Lyme Regis, she is now pioneering community acting and establishing the Colway Theatre Trust.

1970 – 1 May.   An RAF Canberra bomber has crashed into the sea at Lyme Bay during target-towing trials. Two of the crew were killed and one rescued.

1970   Six trawlers and four shell-fish potting boats are operating from West Bay.

1970   Offshore in Lyme Bay you may frequently observe what may seem to be the mating habits of oil tankers. Here the great tankers from the Gulf twin-up with a lesser breed. "Lightening" is the procedure pioneered by Shell in which the partial unloading of crude oil from supertankers of the 250,000 tonne range takes place into smaller vessels. This causes the big ships to rise sufficiently in the water to enable them to enter British harbours. The coast off Lyme Regis was chosen because it is the most sheltered water in the approaches to Britain from the south-west, being protected by the projecting coasts of Start Point and Portland.

1971 – 16 November.   Monkton Wyld, the £180-a-term co-educational boarding school near Charmouth, was today raided by drugs squad officers. They questioned some of the 61 pupils and took away "various substances". Some pupils were also allegedly interviewed about sexual activities and the diary of a 14-year-old girl was removed.

1971 – November.   Customers from the Marshwood vale packed the Bottle Inn, Marshwood, to celebrate the retirement of Bill Stevens on his 65th birthday. They gave him a cheque for £124 and a specially bound book with hundreds of tributes. He has been a baker's roundsman in the Vale since 1921 when he delivered bread from a pony and trap. Mrs R. B. Briscoe of the Mothers' Union told him: "By your selfless loyal service you have achieved the status of an ambassador of peace and goodwill. No crowned head or prime minister could wish for higher praise."

1971 – 10 December.   Thirty-six parents of children at Monkton Wyld school, near Charmouth, condemned police action at the school, which was raided last month. They attended a protest meeting at the school which passed a vote of confidence in the six teachers and expressed "extreme dismay" at the manner the police inquiries were carried out.

1971 – 7 November.   A feature in the Sunday Times celebrates the "Bridport Knot" and points out that more are made in Bridport in a day than a troop of Boy Scouts ties in a year: "One hundred million of them between the time the knotmakers clock on in the morning and off in the evening. It is really one basic knot made over and over again. The Boy Scouts – and other students of the oldest of all man's methods of fastening – would recognise it as a sheet bend. Whether you call it that, or the Bridport Knot, a world-wide business is based upon it. For perhaps a thousand years or more the inhabitants of this Dorset town have employed their cunning of hand to make it, and throughout all that time the town's fortunes and their livings have largely depended upon it. Having a sheet bend like that is as good as money in the bank."

1971 – 15 December.   The slippery surface of a tarred section of Roman road near Compton Valence has been blamed at an inquest in Dorchester today for the death of a rider who fell from her horse. It slipped whilst Mrs Margaret Birley of Hyde Crook, Frampton, was hunting with the Cattistock hounds. She suffered a fractured skull and died the following morning. Other riders had warned her that the road was "like glass".

1972   A rough-cut piece of timber, set in the blue lias-stone wall of a Coombe Street house, in Lyme Regis, has been claimed as Britain's oldest letterbox. It is set beside the bottom left-hand corner of a downstairs window and is the size of half a railway sleeper. There are both horizontal and upright slots. The latter, the top one, was for the benefit of those on horseback. Originally this upper slot was horizontal but it was re-cut into a vertical one for ease of its mounted users.

1973 – 23 May.   Television anchorman and naturalist Kenneth Allsop kills himself with a drugs overdose at his Milton Mill home in the deep-cut valley west of Powerstock, three miles north-east of Bridport. He was suffering chronic pain from an amputated leg, lost in a sporting accident over hurdles while training for wartime service in the Royal Air Force, and faced other medical problems. [A letter was later released into the public domain stating the reasons he had "a deadline to keep" and lamenting man's abuse of the Earth, in particular blaming toxic pollution from agricultural chemicals for the demise of the Peregrine falcon which he had watched on the Pembrokeshire coast a couple of weeks before. Ironically, its decline would be reversed, and the birds returned to breed on the island of Steep Holm, between Weston-super-Mare and Cardiff, which was bought as a nature reserve memorial to Kenneth Allsop in 1976.]

1974   The village school at Thorncombe, in west Dorset, has been burnt to the ground.

1974   Stokewater House, the large Victorian workhouse to the west of Beaminster, which stands just inside the Stoke Abbott parish boundary, is being converted into flats. The building was bought from Dorset County Council, in April 1972, by Spicer (Electrical) Limited for £15,000.

1975 – 3 May.   The closure has taken place of Dorset's last branch railway, with the departure of the 20.40 hours passenger train from Bridport. It is being driven by Reg Chappell, from Westbury Depot, and left to the sounds of alarm-warning detonators placed on the line. Arrived at Maiden Newton, the junction station nine and a quarter miles up the line, was logged at 21.02. [The track would be lifted in 1977.]

1978   Novelist and playwright Thomas Ridley Sharpe [born 1928] has moved to 170 St Andrew's Road, Bridport, from Cambridge. His first farce, *Riotous Assembly* [1971], was followed by some of the most successful books of the decade – *Indecent Exposure* [1973], *Porterhouse Blues* [1974], *Blott on the Landscape* [1975], *Wilt* [1976], *The Great Pursuit* [1977], followed by *The Throwback* this year, and *The Wilt Alternative* in production. [At Bridport he completed *Ancestral Vices*, to the distractions of a plot that was ironically turning into reality as the Bridport Bypass gouged its Blott in a close encounter with his 1.5-acre garden. He left the town.]

1978 – December.   The strange story has unfolded of murdered dissident Georgi Ivanov Markov [1929-78] who was born in Sofia and is buried in Whitchurch Canonicorum churchyard. His stone records that the novelist and playwright died "In the cause of freedom" and was Bulgaria's most revered dissident". On one side of the stone the wording is in English and the other Bulgarian. Though in exile, based in London, Markov continued to be well known inside his homeland for a series of revelatory radio programmes, on the BBC World Service and for the West German-based Radio Free Europe. The Russian KGB is said to have provided Bulgaria's secret agents with the means for implementing Bulgarian Communist Party general secretary Tudor Zhivkov's execution order on the emigré broadcaster in September 1978. As he waited for a bus on Waterloo Bridge an assassin brushed against him and prodded his right thigh with a gas-gun disguised as an umbrella. This injected a pin-head sized pellet containing a lethal quantity of the toxic poison ricin, extracted from castor-oil seeds. His widow, Annabel Dilke, is from west Dorset and they had a daughter, Sacha.

1979   Richard Fox of Lyme Regis has been voted World Champion Town Crier. [He would retain the title in the following year's competition.]

1979   The 225-acre farm at Labour-in-Vain, west of Abbotsbury, has been accepted by the Treasury in lieu of capital transfer tax from the executors of the late J. R. Bridgman. It will be transferred to the National Trust, through the National Land Fund which was established in memory of those who died in the Second World War.

1980   Lyme Regis railway station has been demolished – and rebuilt at Alresford, near Winchester. The Mid-Hants Railway reopens there on 22 March, and the Edwardian timber buildings and signs from the Dorset seaside will return to the authentic atmosphere of steam working.

1981   Eric Hamblet, the harbourmaster at West Bay, reports only three ships using the port in the past year. Each carried fertilisers. Commercial operations from the harbour are the lowest on record, there being only one trawler and a single pot-boat fishing for lobsters and crabs.

1983 – 21 January. A £7 million Royal Navy Sea Harrier of 899 Naval Air Squadron, on a training flight from RNAS Yeovilton, went out of control above Cattistock at 09.34 hours today, Friday. It narrowly missed homes in West End and Beech Tree Close and crashed into a hedge one field away from the bungalows. No one was hurt. The pilot, 28-year-old Flight Lieutenant Kevin Fox, had ejected safely. Asked about the villagers' reactions, a huntsman told television reporters: "There may be some complaints from old women of both sexes but there are many military families in the area and most of us know that these things are bound to happen from time to time."

1984 – 11 September   [Official report rendered unabridged in order to convey its unfolding drama and filmic potential]. At 18.52 hours the lifeboat station secretary at Lyme Regis was informed by Portland Coastguard that some persons had been cut off by the tide at Black Beach groynes and bodies could be seen in the water. The maroons were fired and at 19.00 the relief *Atlantic-21* rigid inflatable lifeboat was launched with John Hodder at the helm. The wind was north-westerly force three to four with a slight sea. High water was to occur two hours later. Full speed was maintained until the lifeboat reached the area where, due to the groynes, the sea was sweeping in from seaward in a confused manner, causing waves of eight to ten feet high. Three persons and a dog were seen to be stranded at the head of the groyne on stone steps below the sea wall, and could not move because of the depth of the water below and the height of the sea wall above them. A policeman above them was unable to climb down to pull them upwards because of the height of the sea wall. Helmsman John Hodder decided that the two bodies in the water were most at risk, if still alive, and should be rescued first. The lifeboat manoeuvred towards them using the full range of both engines' power and direction to cope with the extraordinarily confused sea. The two bodies, a man and a woman, were pulled aboard and although they appeared lifeless, crew members Robert Irish and James Thomas at once administered first aid and resuscitation, and continued doing so throughout. John Hodder then determined that the other three should be lifted off the head of the groyne immediately, as the tide was rising and they were in danger of being swept off by the sea. The lifeboat approached the head of the groyne and using the full range of power and direction, the stern was positioned between the head of the groyne and the stone steps. The two males appeared to be suffering from exhaustion and the woman indicated with some despair that she could not leave the dog behind. The helmsman was unable to hold the lifeboat in position for more than a few seconds at a time and had to make eight approaches before all three had been successfully heaved aboard by crew member Paul Watson. The policeman above, meanwhile, had been able to grasp the dog's leash and haul it up on to the sea wall. All three survivors were wrapped in thermal sheets and attempts made to warm them by the crew members. The casualties all had to be carried ashore to the waiting ambulance, where the lifeboat station honorary medical adviser pronounced two dead and the other three to be suffering from exposure. The lifeboat made one more trip to the scene to recover a picnic basket and haversack belonging to the casualties. Minor damage had been sustained to the bow of the lifeboat but this was repaired with a patch and the boat was washed down and re-housed at 19.30 hours. John Hodder has been awarded the Royal National Lifeboat Institution's bravery award and crewmen Paul Watson, Robert Irish, and James Thomas have received letters of appreciation.

1985 – 4 February.   The Times diary column reports that a young Dorset lad has no worries for the rest of the millennium. He has booked a table for eight at the Ritz for New Year's Eve – on 31 December 1999.

1985 – 17 February.   The world's largest moth has been loitering in the Natural History Museum in South Kensington, London, for nearly 20 years without anyone knowing. The curators had a perfect excuse for not knowing it was there – as it was locked away inside a lump of 180 million-years-old rock. The specimen of calcareous mudstone in the museum's Jackson collection was found by a Lyme Regis amateur geologist and given to the museum in 1966. The moth, which is 40 million years older than the previous record-holder, in Russia, was found by chance when Paul Whalley, an entomologist at the museum, made what he describes as "a lucky break" in splitting open the rock sample. Whalley plans to call his discovery Archaeolepis, meaning "ancient scales", because of the appearance of its wings. Its closest living relatives are insects of the miscropterygidea group, which include caddis flies.

1986 – September.   West Bay fisherman Jack Woolmington has recovered the anchor of the 30-gun Dutch treasure-ship *Hope* which was plundered on the Chesil Beach, opposite Fleet [16-17 January 1784]. It was found 75 yards offshore and is 14 feet long, rusty, and pebble-encrusted. [It now lies outside the appropriately named Anchor Inn at Chideock.]

1987 – 19 July.   Opening the 130-metres long River Brit Viaduct, which is the centrepiece of the £5 million Bridport Bypass, and aware that the Bridport Brewery was in sight, Roads and Traffic Minister Peter Bottomley came up with an appropriate metaphor: "We have uncorked a bottleneck." The new 7.3-metre single-carriageway, which is 1.8 miles in length and landscaped by 27,000 trees and shrubs, now carries the A35 trunk road, down from the hills at Miles Cross to the B3157 at Sea Road South roundabout.

1989   Old media hands are mourning crime reporter Percy Hoskins [1904-89] who was born in Bridport. For half a century he was Fleet Street's ace sleuth. He was first with the news, for the Daily Express, of the defection to Russia of spies Guy Burgess and Donald Maclean [1951]. Hoskins was alone in championing the defence of Dr John Bodkin Adams, the fashionable Eastbourne doctor who was the victim of press whispers that he had been poisoning wealthy women. The jury agreed that the other hacks were wrong. "Two men have been acquitted today – Adams and Hoskins," Lord Beaverbrook said on 9 April 1957.

1991   Bulgarian President Zhelyu Zhelev today paid homage, in the pouring rain, beside the Dorset grave of murdered dissident Georgi Markov [1929-78] in Whitchurch Canonicorum churchyard. "This crime was a great shame to our country," he said.

1992 – 10 January.   Listeners to the "Today" programme on Radio 4 were treated to Nellie Templeton, in her eighties, playing the music for silent films in the Regent Theatre at Lyme Regis – in the 1990s as she had in the 1920s. Her lush piano mood renderings are entirely from memory and played without looking at the keyboard. This was not only so that she followed each frame of the film but came about because of the total darkness of the early picture houses which caused her to learn to play-blind.

1992 – 11 March.   The body of Down's syndrome sufferer Jo Ramsden [1969-91] who disappeared from an adult training centre in Bridport on 9 April 1991, has been discovered in woodland at Raymond's Hill, Wootton Fitzpaine, on the hill above Lyme Regis, by Forestry Commission workers. She had last been seen crossing the road in Bridport with "a young man in a bright patterned jumper" and her decomposed remains were found accompanied by a Liverpool football bag and multi-coloured tracksuit of the type she had been wearing at the time of her disappearance.

1992   A 65-feet reef of sunset coral, discovered two miles off Lyme Regis, is only the third that is known around Britain's coast, the others being in Plymouth Sound and off Lundy Island. The species is at the northern end of its range in the southern British Isles, being dependent upon warm water.

1993 – 20 March.   Tragedy unfolded across the cold waters of Lyme Bay this Monday afternoon. Two instructors, eight sixth-formers from Plymouth, and their teacher, had set off in canoes from a Lyme Regis activity centre shortly after 10.00 hours. They paddled eastwards and were then intending to turn inshore, to land at Charmouth, with 13.00 being given as the estimated time of arrival. Nothing was done about their failure to reach land and Portland Coastguards were unaware of any canoeists out at sea until they received a radio call from the West Bay fishing boat *Spanish Eyes* at 14.43: "Portland, we've picked-up an empty canoe." At 14.58 the Coastguards establish that a party had left Lyme five hours earlier. A Land Rover is sent to coastal viewpoints to try and make visual contact. They can see nothing. Almost an hour later, at 15.51, the Coastguards scramble the first of two Royal Navy Sea-King air-sea rescue helicopters from RNAS Portland. They arrive on the scene, about 17 miles north-west from their base, at 16.08. Coastguards then launch Lyme's *Atlantic 21* inshore lifeboat, at 16.11, and a rescue team from All Hallows public school also head towards the search area. Meanwhile, at 16.29, the St Alban's Adventure Centre in Lyme identify the canoe recovered by the Bridport fishing boat, and confirm that it belongs to the group from Southway Comprehensive School. A yellow Royal Air Force Wessex rescue helicopter is scrambled from RAF Chivenor in north Devon. At 17.17 HMS *Beaver* sends her Lynx helicopter to join the aerial search. By 17.38 the Lyme lifeboat has found survivors and is hauling two adults aboard, alive though suffering from hypothermia, and they are taken to West Bay, from where a helicopter takes them to hospital. At 17.43 a Sea King picks-up another canoeist, a mile east of Lyme Regis, followed by three others, by 17.55. They are delivered to Weymouth General Hospital at 18.00. Minutes later, at 18.04, the RAF Wessex helicopter reports that it has picked up four more. Finally, at 18.44, the second Sea King picks up the last canoeist, who is still breathing, nearly nine hours after they set off and eight hours after they got into difficulties. Questions are asked about how they went to sea without notifying the Coastguards or carrying a marine-band radio for just such an emergency. Had they undertaken capsize drill? Why non-arrival at Charmouth had not been reported when they failed to come into sight at 13.00? On the credit side, wetsuits and lifejackets were being worn, and distress flares carried, though none appears to have been fired. Had the helicopters been sent at the earliest opportunity? The prolonged nature of the search has taken its toll. Four teenagers were pulled from the sea either dead or dying and are named as Simon Dunne (16), Claire Langley (16), Dean Sayer (17), and Rachel Walker (16).

1993 – 29 October.   Golfing legend Group Captain George Houghton [1905-93], author of the *Golf Addict* books and 50 other titles, has died at Bridport. He lived at Coneygar House and the flag at Bridport Golf Club is flying at half-mast in tribute.

1995   Additional   acquisitions   over   recent   years   have consolidated National Trust ownership of the coast between Lyme Regis and Eype. The Golden Cap Estate now totals 1,974 acres, mostly in a contiguous block of land five miles wide. Outlying holdings consist of the isolated heather-clad summit of Hardown Hill and the dramatic mudflows and landslips of Black Venn and the Spittles. The only significant gaps are around the village of Charmouth and at Seatown hamlet.

1998   "Harbour Lights", starring Nick Berry of "Heartbeat" fame, is filmed at West Bay and is set to do for the west Dorset coast what ITV's heart-throb has achieved for the picturesque North Yorkshire village of Goathland. Berry is the harbourmaster and co-stars with Tina Hobley from Coronation Street. Expect Nick Berry fridge magnets and similar offerings in souvenir shops as coachloads of fans abandon Hollywood-on-the-Moors for the delights of the Dorset seaside.

Old Lyme

Armada times: pictorial defence map showing 'the Cobb of Lyme' (top), Lyme town (centre), Charmouth (left), and a beacon blazing on Timber Hill.

Target towing: firing off the first shots of a new war, in the Royal Navy's Lyme Bay gunnery ranges, from HMS *Agamemnon* in August 1914.

Speed trials: newly-built destroyers HMS *Tyrian* and HMS *Tetrarch* in Lyme Bay, at the end of the Great War.

Final photograph: the battleship HMS *Formidable*, seen from HMS *Agamemnon*, hours before she was sunk by a German torpedo, off Lyme Regis.

Defiant message: 'HMS *Formidable.* Are We Downhearted? 1st Jan 1915.' Survivors photographed on HMS *Agamemnon*, by Captain G. C. C. Crookshank.

Lyme landing: the Duke of Monmouth, who arrived to claim the Stuart throne and instead lost his head.

Lyme's villain: Judge Jeffreys, whose Bloody Assize in 1685, in retribution for the Monmouth Rebellion, led to twelve gruesome executions on the beach west of the Cobb.

Lyme smuggler: jailed in 1832 at Dorchester, Jack Rattenbury emerged to write his memoirs and become a romantic hero.

Fossil lady: the formidable Mary Anning, with faithful Troy at her side, as she now hangs in the Natural History Museum.

Town crying: by now there must be a law against such ear-bending deafening
as displayed by Richard Fox, World Champion Town Crier of 1979-80.

Civilising influence: two young ladies find there is a quieter side to Richard
Fox, freshly arrived in New Orleans.

Lyme's author: John Fowles at his Belmont House home, photographed by Colin Graham and Rodney Legg in 1973.

VIEW OF THE LANDSLIP
about one mile to the Eastward of the great Chasm at Dowlar

ANDS ,

'ace on the 3rd of February 1840.

Great landslip: cottage at the foot of Whitlands Cliff in 1840, drawn by William Dawson.

Landslip Cottage: the famous house that changed its grid reference, fortunately before the concept was invented.

Coast road: eastwards out of Lyme, across what are now the landslipped National Trust properties of The Spittles and Black Ven.

Marine Parade: suffering a double whammy from sodden clay and an angry sea, on 5 December 1926.

Little landslip: what the estate agents now have to tell us about Lyme Regis, seen on 6 April 1963 (with the house being subsequently righted).

Lost road: now one of the most desolate landscapes in Britain, across the landslipped Spittles and Black Venn.

Active mudslide: on the cliffs towards Charmouth, having carried away the public path into the sea.

Marine Parade: the Victorian link between ancient Lyme and its mediaeval Cobb harbour, with Wings being the white house in the middle.

Negative evidence: Wings and the linking promenade to the Cobb being absent in this Daniel Dunster painting of 1832-33.

Councillors' folly: weather-boarded Wings (centre) on the site of which Lyme dignitaries erected a plaque stating Jane Austen had stayed there, while ignoring evidence it had not even been built at the time of her visit.

Lyme quay: the main berth at the Cobb harbour, painted in the 1840s.

Cobb harbour: seen in the 1890s, with the coaster 'Glencoe' having brought in coal and to leave with cement made on the western shore from the local lias stone. Note the tennis courts above the houses, on the level ground below the landslipped slopes.

Calm sea: the classic Colin Graham photograph of a misty morn from the southern arm of the Cobb (notorious now for its breaking waves in the John Fowles film).

Heavy seas: Lyme Regis at the Buddle estuary, looking eastwards to Golden Cap (centre) and Thorncombe Beacon.

Angry sea: tossing the ships moored off the Buddle estuary and Gun Cliff in 1832, painted by Charles Marshall.

Lyme nudes: the George Cruickshank caricature aroused such passions in wannabe sedate Lyme Regis, as one hardly imagines it was in Jane Austen's time.

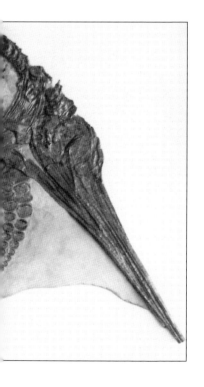

Lyme fossil: the sort of sealife that would be producing television programmes today if Earth had not been hit by an asteroid 65 million years ago.

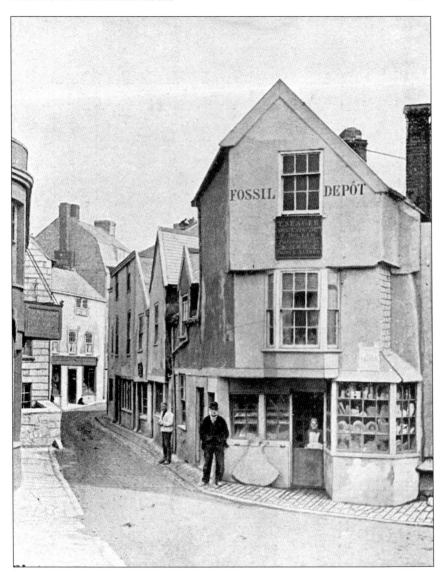

Fossil shop: Mary Anning's depot, at the bottom of the main street in Lyme Regis, where she was born and started her business.

Giant ammonite: typical specimen from the Jurassic coast, now common as architectural features.

Lyme's blacksmith: in photographs as well as in oils, Samuel Govier presented an irresistible image at the 'Little Forge' as James Abbott McNeill Whistler called it (now Woolworths).

**The blacksmith: Samuel Govier, as immortalised in a lithograph by
J. A. M. Whistler.**

Fanny Adams: standing (right, in black dress) at the front door of the cottages fronting the forge, where Woolworths now stands.

Little Forge: Whistler's painting features Samuel Govier at work.

Lyme Sunday: looking up Broad Street, a century before seven day trading, in a lithograph by J. A. M. Whistler.

Main street: looking up Broad Street, Lyme Regis circa 1880, with a pre-royal Lion Hotel and Hawker's New Inn (right).

Overnight stay: the Royal Field Artillery, en route to Okehampton and the Dartmoor ranges, broke their journey at Lyme (Broad Street and the old Drill Hall, later Marine Theatre) in 1888.

Cobb Road: Holm Lea Terrace and the house from which Captain Sir Richard Spencer went off to found Albany, Western Australia.

Thatched mill: the Upper Mill on the River Lim, with its wheel preserved beneath the tiled canopy.

Rustic touch: protective shelter for the mill-wheel where Dorset meets Devon.

Coaching inn: the Old
Monmouth Hotel sets out its
history on the wall, including
the Duke of Monmouth's
cavalry and Oscar Wilde, who
signed a window pane.

Lyme's Jordan: the post-1660 Restoration Baptist 'sanctuary' on the edge of Lyme borough, with Monkey's Rough (centre) and Higher Mill (behind). Fields to the left of the river Lim are known as Paradise, Little Paradise and Jericho. From a watercolour by I. Mortimer, 1924.

Jericho cottages: the old Baptists named the spots along the River Lim where they immersed their converts with scriptural aptness, such as Jordan, Jericho and Paradise.

Rustic quarters: Monkey's Rough, a cottage in Jericho.

Street boys: Sherborne Lane at Lyme Regis at the turn of the 20th century.

Flood damage: viewing the aftermath of the flash-flood of Whitsun 1890, beside Town Mills (centre) which became the town's electrical power station.

Lyme flood: the double levels of the River Lim, having run as one after the cloudburst on Whit Sunday in 1890, seen beside the Angel Inn.

The Lynch: beside the River Lim, down from the Angel Inn at Lyme Regis.

BOROUGH OF LYME REGIS

A Schedule of Tolls Payable to the Corporation of Lyme Regis in respect of Goods and Merchandise for Sale.

For a Front Stall in the Butchers Market, per week ~ ~ ~ ~ 1/6	For every person Hawking on Foot 1°
For a Back Stall in ditto, per week 1/3	For Pigs, each ~ ~ ~ ~ ~ ~ 2°
For every Butcher Hawking Meat 1/0	For every Bull, Bullock, Cow or Heifer ~ 3°
For each Stall at a Fair ~ ~ ~ 1/6	For every Calf ~ ~ ~ ~ ~ ~ 1°
For Two Stalls ditto kept by the same person 2/0	For every Sheep per Score and in proportion for less or more than a Score ~ 5°
For a Nut Stall at ditto ~ ~ ~ 6°	For every Horse, Mule or Ass ~ ~ 6°
For Swings etc. at ditto, each ~ 6°	For every Stall in the Fish Market ~ 3°
For Goods Pitched ~ ~ ~ ~ ~ 1/0	For every Boat with Fish ~ ~ ~ 3°
For every Brush or Hardware Van ~ 6°	For every Trawler with Fish under 20 tons 6°
For every person Hawking Goods by Cart, Waggon, Horse, Mule or Ass 2°	For every Trawler with Fish 20 tons and above ~ ~ ~ ~ 1/-

By Order of the Council,
Borough of Lyme Regis.

HENRY HENLEY
Mayor
20th. May 1872

Market charges: Lymes tolls of 1872, when you could have landed your 20-ton trawler for a shilling.

Sun Insurance: their 1710-dated fire engine on its last shout, against impossible odds at a devastating fire in Broad Street, Lyme Regis, in 1889.

First car: to have a Lyme owner, being the De Dion Bouton with R. Wallace at the wheel and Spike Hardy having a ride, in 1902.

Eastern view: Lyme and the Cobb, seen from the Spittles in about 1900.

Lobster pots: belonging to the Curtis family, on what used to be the eastern fishery, on former Church Beach, seen in the 1880s.

Coast defences: gun-guard for the late 20th-century extension of Lyme's promenade across the former Church Beach, with a view of Golden Cap.

Classic views: the Cobb and its outer arm, which has a sloping top and was never designed for a romantic walk into the spray.

Oall Rite Ansum!

A Salute to Cornish Dialect

Les Merton

with illustrations by Richard Scollins

COUNTRYSIDE BOOKS
NEWBURY BERKSHIRE

COUNTRYSIDE BOOKS
3 Catherine Road
Newbury, Berkshire

To view our complete range of books,
please visit us at
www.countrysidebooks.co.uk

ISBN 978 1 85306 814 0

Designed by Peter Davies, Nautilus Design
Produced through MRM Associates Ltd., Reading
Typeset by CJWT Solutions, St Helens
Printed by Cambridge University Press

*All material for the manufacture of this book
was sourced from sustainable forests.*

CONTENTS

ACKNOWLEDGEMENTS

Special thanks to the following:

All the staff at The Cornwall Centre, Redruth
The Federation of Old Cornwall Societies
Redruth Museum, Helston Museum, Bodmin Museum
Joy Stevenson, who first inspired me to write in dialect
Nicola Clark, John Berryman, Mike Osman, Mark Kaczmarek, Ron White and all
   those who have played a part in putting this book together

Author's Note
In this book, words may occasionally be spelt differently to allow for the different
accents in Cornwall.

FOREWORD

I am very pleased to add this article as a foreword to this book of Cornish dialect.

One sign of change in Cornwall has been the decline of our lovely old dialect. However, when two or more Cornish people meet to chat it is still very much in evidence, with its own vocabulary, individual sounds of vowel and consonant and the very special way these are woven into phrases and sentences. Despite analytic and phonological investigations our dialect defies linguistic and grammatical rules and simply remains a unique, indigenous form of spoken word handed down from generation to generation.

Over the many years I have recorded our dialect I sometimes feel that dialect recorders, speakers and writers are looked on as licensed fools. Certainly there have been times when I am led to believe that work on dialect is not important, especially in the eyes of linguistic snobs. This has never bothered me because I know that our dialect is a part of our heritage which enshrines the very spirit of Cornwall and is as important as our old crosses, standing stones and cromlechs. The day we no longer hear the rich sounds of it will be the death knell of a Cornishness which can never be resurrected or put in a museum.

The sad thing is that in the 20th century our dialect was banished from the classrooms by educationalists, and children were made to feel inferior when they spoke in broad dialect. I well remember a girl in my class at school saying: 'I would like to learn French, Miss.' She was told in a sarcastic manner: 'My dear child you can't speak English yet.' I have never forgotten the tears welling up in the girl's eyes.

Many got rid of their dialect and some almost became ashamed of the way their parents spoke. Children were told that certain words were only fit for people who aspired to no higher than menial jobs all their lives. The deliberate act of omitting to tell us that we once had our own language from which many of our dialect words came has a lot to answer for.

Cornish self-esteem was eroded and too many Cornish tried to ape the English accent. For some reason they got the feeling that sounding 'English' made them superior in some way. This is an attitude I have never understood and luckily have never suffered from. I was brought up to be proud not only to be Cornish but to sound Cornish.

Many countries are so proud of their dialects. The old Venetian speech can be heard in the medieval town of Marostica near Venice, for instance. In the town square is a huge chess board where the moves are called out in their old dialect as the human chess pieces move. Yet in this country we seem obsessed with the idea of getting rid of regional accents and replacing them with flavourless English.

Dominated as we are by experts and literal facts, we are also fast losing the habit of instant metaphor which comes so naturally to dialect speakers. For whatever the faults and limitations of dialect it is a language which, though down to earth, gives scope to the imagination found in no other form of speaking or writing. We all know people who speak in a pompous manner for two hours yet say nothing, but this is impossible when speaking Cornish dialect as it has the delicious inborn quality to deflate pretentious pomposity – one reason why I love it so much.

Some criticise the grammar in Cornish dialect and I maintain that the sacred grammatical maxims have no place in our dialect. It is a speech form and speech was with us long before grammar. I think Sir Arthur Quiller Couch got it right when he said: 'Cornishmen are bilingual, they can speak dialect or English.' We are lucky we can speak both, yet too many neglect their dialect and it will be lost if we don't use it.

A 'cultured' Cornishman or woman is a supreme example of the oxymoron 'falsely true', and sums up for me any Cornish who exclude their dialect. Too many write books on Cornwall, shout from the rooftops that they are Cornish and carry around their family tree, yet have worked deliberately to eliminate the one thing which is essentially Cornish – their dialect.

An interesting study published by *Mintel* recently about the regeneration of regional accents describes a marked cultural phenomenon. Some areas becoming run down and depressed have developed a 'dog in the manger' provincialism which makes them reject anything to do with the prosperous South East, including its accent.

Isn't it odd that despite Cornwall being more depressed than most in this century, it seems to have taken the opposite view and rejected its own lovely dialect? How can a race of people as ancient and proud as the Cornish allow their unique dialect to die? It is so full of remnants of our old language, has so much humour. Even when speaking English many Cornish mean something quite different from the actual words they utter, giving rise to blank looks whilst the Cornish grizzle in their pasties.

Recording Cornish dialect soon dispels any idea that one is an expert. The essence of an expert is man yearning to be God. You soon realise this is not so when speaking perhaps to an old lady in a small village who puts you firmly in

your place with the remark: 'Aw, we dawnt say un like that up ere, me ansum.' My message to all the Cornish is: don't deny your identity, use your rich dialect as often as you can and pass it on to your children. Use it or lose it, but never be ashamed of it. I shall always use it and promote it. It is part of the wonderful diversity of accents found in this island of ours.

If you are reading Cornish dialect aloud for the first time from the phonetically written dialect in this book or if you are born and bred Cornish always speak it with pride.

Joy Stevenson (Maid Lowenna)
(Bard of The Cornish Gorsedd)

8

INTRODUCTION

While I hope you find this book both amusing and entertaining, the underlying reason for its existence is, in fact, a serious one. My intention is to put into print, for modern readers, something of the fast disappearing dialect of the region – 'Cornish dialect' by name and nature.

The book does not pretend to be either a comprehensive study of dialect or a detailed local history. However, I do believe that the variety of subject matter reflects the real Cornwall and, most important of all, the dialect expresses the warmth and humour that are so much part of the Cornish personality.

This project reflects something of the character of the born and bred Cornish I grew up with and still live alongside in Cornwall. It has been enhanced further by the study of books on dialect, listening to audio tapes and by specially conducted interviews. Apart from the facts gleaned in this way, most of this book comes from personal experience. I speak dialect naturally and I'm always amazed when, looking at it closely like this, I find many words that I considered to be English are in fact Cornish dialect.

There is one very special point about Cornish dialect – some of the words survived or were derived from Kernewek (the Cornish language) when the language was considered to be lost. Dialect words with their Kernewek links are listed in the glossary.

This is probably the appropriate time to write briefly about the language known as Cornish or Kernewek. It is one of the Brythonic group of Celtic languages, closely linked to Breton and less closely to Welsh. This is illustrated in the following table of Celtic language groups.

Goidelic	**Brythonic**
Irish Gaelic – Scotch Gaelic – Manx	Welsh – Cornish – Breton

Kernewek was spoken throughout Cornwall till about the year 1400. By 1600 English had driven it west of Truro. Dolly Pentreath who died in 1777 is reputed to be the last Cornish speaker. However, there is evidence that the Cornish language lingered well into the 19th century.

Andrew Borde in his *Boke of the Introduction of Knowledge*, published in 1542, states, 'In Cornwall is two speches, the one is naughty englyshe, and the other is

Cornysshe speche.' This quote emphasises the existence and gradual decline of Cornish language; being a dialect enthusiast I love to think 'naughty englyshe' refers to a dialect of the times.

The main concern of this book is to record the everyday dialect speech of Cornwall. I make no apology for concentrating mainly on the full traditional dialect rather than a watered-down modern version. In fact, although this extreme form of dialect may be on its way out, there are pockets of resistance, and not every dialect speaker is elderly.

I consider myself lucky that I still hear the sounds, in my head, of the rich Cornish dialect of my country childhood. This obviously reflects in my speech. 'Yew tawk awful broad.' This remark was made to me recently at a dialect performance, by Cornish Bard and leading dialect authority Joy Stevenson, meaning I talk in full dialect.

In the reporting of everyday speech two words frequently occur, dialect and accent, and since these two words may seem to be loosely applied at times, we ought to define the difference between them at this stage. In simple terms, accent is a matter of pronunciation, whereas dialect involves vocabulary, special phrases, and even a different grammar. When we speak of a person's accent, we usually mean that he is speaking what is known as 'Standard English', but with distinctive features of pronunciation. Stanley Ellis, an expert in dialect from Leeds University, puts it like this: 'Dialect is a traditionally-developed correct way of speaking from the area in which it is used; accent is an attempt at speaking the standard language and modifying it in the local sort of manner.'

An example of this is the word *till*, meaning to cultivate; in Cornish dialect this is pronounced *teal* (rhyme with meal). In Cornwall, farmers *teal tatties en tha field*.

It is also worth noting that everyone has his or her own way of speaking – we all talk a kind of personal dialect. Sometimes families have small dialect patterns of their own, a few words or phrases which carry a meaning for those 'in the know', and the same can be said of social groups from Rugby Clubs to Women's Institutes. At the same time, we tend to be inconsistent in the way we use language; within the space of a couple of sentences a speaker may well pronounce the same word in several different ways. It is also common knowledge that the way we speak varies according to the company we are in.

When referring to Cornish dialect we are generalising; these days dialect and accent are not as strictly confined to a small area as they used to be. Gone are the days when one small area talked in a different dialect and accent from another small area in Cornwall. At one time residents of a town like Penryn could be identified by their accent by a resident of St Ives and vice versa.

However, using a simple example of counting to ten I have illustrated, by writing phonetically, the different sounds of the numbers as spoken that may be encountered:

English	Dialect
naught	aught
one	wawn, wan, wun
two	tew, toe, tow, dew
three	dree, thray
four	fower, vower
five	vyve, fi-ve
six	zix
seven	zebben, sebben
eight	ite, aite, ate
nine	nyne, ni-nne
ten	tane, tin

There are other things that occur that cannot even be written phonetically yet they are still a very important part of expression in dialect. A Cornishman has a distinctive way of agreeing or saying 'yes' which cannot be spelt or written. This is achieved by holding the teeth a little apart, with the mouth rounded, a short and quick intake of breath creates a sibilance. This short hissing sound is meant for 'yes' and is in fact the equivalent of a nod.

Cornwall is the most south-westerly county of England with over two hundred miles of coastline exposed to the sea and with the River Tamar as another distinct boundary (it is only joined to Devon by a small strip of land). For all facts and purposes it is another country or an island, especially as far as dialect goes. This makes the criterion used to establish the area of its dialect far simpler to define than an area of dialect in other parts of England.

The higher social status of Standard English inevitably led to a movement to correct the speech of dialect areas. In Cornwall, schoolchildren were encouraged to *talk proper* and not always by gentle means. The arrival of national broadcasting and later of television all played their part in the demise of dialect.

The truth is that, whilst a standard form of English is useful as a kind of dictionary to which we can refer, or use as a point of comparison, and whilst it obviously makes communication between different parts of the English-speaking world much easier, there is no question of it being more correct than other forms of English. No way of speaking is intrinsically right or wrong, despite all the misguided attempts by generations of teachers and preachers to exterminate all localised forms of speech and frequent exhortations to children to 'scrape their tongues'. There is much evidence that attempts by educators to eradicate dialect speech have continued almost unabated, often despite official advice to the contrary: 'Teachers should not consider themselves in any sense called upon to extirpate a genuine local dialect' (*Teachers' Handbook*, 1929, page 74).

With this last quote in mind let's look at the way this book is written. The dialect is transcribed phonetically in as straightforward a way as possible and with the simplest spellings in the belief that if it is read aloud it will preserve the sound and tradition of the dialect.

Doan't worray me ansums, yew waon't bay piskey led.

Les Merton

Humpty Dumpty

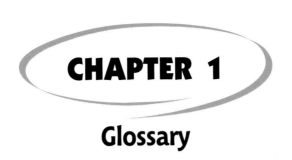

CHAPTER 1

Glossary

This glossary falls broadly into two sections: a list of words and expressions, arranged alphabetically, and a series of other entries, grouped under classified headings. I have mixed words and phrases, and include some non-standard pronunciations as well as unusual dialect features.

I have also included more modern dialect expressions along with those which are now quite rare; and have tried not to look upon the older ones with exaggerated sentimentality, though I do believe it is worth a special effort to record, and perhaps even preserve, some of the more traditional and fast-disappearing dialect phrases.

Any glossary of this type must be incomplete; many readers may well know examples other than those included here, or may even doubt whether some entries are in common use today.

Abroad   Open.

Naw wondur thay scor'd, tha goalie ad es legs wide abroad
                   No wonder they scored, the goalkeeper had his legs wide apart.

Tha dore es abroad
                   The door is open.

Afeerd   Afraid.

I wudden bit afeerd
                   I wasn't afraid.

Anchunt/Ancient   Said of a child, meaning they are quaint or old fashioned.

Sha's sum anchunt

Ansum   Good, well, healthy. Ansum is also a term of endearment.

Arfurr   Refers to King Arthur. His spirit was incarnated in the chough.

Ass/Arse   Back side.

Ass about faace Wrong way round.

Avore	Before.
Awkerd	Awkward.

Sha's awkerd lik a cow andlun a musket
> She's awkward like a cow handling a musket.

Ax, Ax'd	Ask, Asked.
Barra	To borrow.
Backlong	Before, in days gone by.
Baissly/Baisslay	Dirty.

Ur plaace waas baissly
> Her place was dirty.

Bealed	When the bill of a chick pokes through a hatching egg.
Betterun	Health is improving, getting better from an illness.

Bettur fit I staid ome
> It would be better if I stayed at home.

Betturmost	People further up the social scale.
Bustguts	Someone who is greedy.
Caall ome	Can't remember.

I knaw en, but I caant caall en ome
> I know him but I can't remember who he is.

Caggled	Covered.
Chrismuss curl	Christmas carol.
Clunk	To swallow.
Coose	To chase.
Cram	A white lie, a likely story.
Cum-mis-zon	An invitation, come on.
Dabber'd	Soiled by mud.

Es trowsies es dabber'd
> His trousers are covered in mud.

Daggin/Daggun	Longing to do something.
Dam	Secure.

Sittun es tight es a dam
> Sitting very secure.

Dear obem	Dear of him. Expression of endearment.

Dinyan/Didjan   A little corner, a small portion. A didjan of pasty was left to appease the knockers (little people) down the mines.

Dob   To throw or fling.

Dribbling/Dribblun   Dripping, running

Tha chield's nawse es dribblun lik snaw owt ov a barrul

The child's nose is running like snow out of a barrel.

Droll teller   A story teller.

Ef   If.

Ef yew wur ta dew es yew oft ta dew, yew wud dew a gud deal bettur than yew dew dew

If you were to do as you ought to do, you would do a good deal better than you do do.

Ent   To pour.

Euchred   Cornered, beaten (from the card game of euchre).

Faate   Fête.

Gwain ta tha faate

Going to the fête.

Fairings   Biscuits.

Fert   Anus.

Ur faace waas screw'd up lik a duck's fert

Her face was screwed up like a duck's anus.

Fi-er inyun   Fire engine.

Flam new   Brand new.

Flummixed   Perplexed.

Flushed   Plenty of money.

Frame up   Adopt a fighting posture.

Full ov et   Full of mischief.

Furriner   Foreigner.

Furst class   Top of the range.

Gaape   To look with an open mouth.

Gaate pos chield   Gate post child. Illegitimate.

Gaddle   To drink greedily.

Geek   To look. *Gyky* is Kernewek for 'to peep'.

Geet	Big.
Geeze daincin	A Christmas play in which the players obscure their identity.
Giss on	To doubt what someone is saying. To be dismissive, as in 'Don't talk rubbish'.
Gwain un lik a long dog	
	Running like a greyhound.
Handsum	Handsome, pleasant, fine.
Ow ee do-un my/me handsum?	
	How are you my handsome?
Henderment/Hinderment	
	Obstruction, delay, hindrance.
Ee's oall-waays under my feet n hinderun me	
	He's always under my feet and hindering me.
Hitch'd up	Children not looked after, like a horse hitched and left.
Housing	To go house to house gossiping.
Iss	Yes.
Isself	Himself.
Jant	Jaunt.
Johnny Fortnight	Packman, door to door peddlar.
Kaip	Keep.
Kell	Kill.
Kennee/Kennay?	Can you?
Kewse	To talk.
Kiddly	Milk sops or food for invalids.
Kilter	State, dilemma.
Mawthur waas en sum kilter. Sha sid, 'Kennee kaip owt or shell I ave ta kell yew ta git a bit ov payce.'	
	Mother was in some state. She said, 'Can you keep out or shall I have to kill you to get a bit of peace.'
Labbet	Labourer, drudge.
Lagg'd	Dirty, mud-stained, unwashed.
Lam	To hit.
I reallay lamm'd inta en	
	I really hit him.

Leak	Drop.
I'll av a leak ov tay	
	I'll have a drop of tea.
Lerraps	Rags, shreds, bits.
Es shurt waas torn ta lerraps	
	His shirt was torn to shreds.
Lickurs	Large ones.
Lor a massy	Lord have mercy.
Lowster	To do manual labour.
Lummux	Fool.
Maid/Maiden	Girl.
Manshuns	Small loaves of bread, baked without tins. Eccentric Cornish preacher Billy Bray is reputed to have said, 'You won't go hungry when you get to heaven for in God's house there are many *manshuns*.'
Mazzed	Angry.
Ee waas mazzed	
	He was angry.
Mind	To remember, recall.
Do ee mind Ivor Pascoe?	
	Do you remember Ivor Pascoe?
Mygar	Surprise, my gosh, my God.
New vang	New thing or novelty.
Thay theer mobal phones es a new vang, but I doant see um catchun un	
	Those mobile phones are a novelty but I can't see them getting established.
Nicey	Sweets.
Ef yew be-ave yew caan ave a bit ov nicey	
	If you behave you can have some sweets.
Nite craw	Night crow, said of a person who is active at night.
Noisiz	Noises.
Nuff	Enough.
I've ad nuff ta ate, any more an I'll be blawd up like a pig	
	I've had enough to eat, any more and I'll be as fat as a pig.

Odds et   To alter, to make a difference.

  Caan't odds et   Can't make a difference.

Oald/Old   Can mean musty as well as old.

  They books da smell old.
                     Those books smell musty.

Owt un a limb   Taking a chance, as in out on a weak branch on a tree.

Pard   Friend, mate, partner if working with someone.

Party   Girl.

  I'll gwain owt weth thus party down et Port-lebben
                     I'm going out with this girl down at Porthleven. The terms
                     down and up are often attached to places. I go up to St
                     Austell, for example.

Passel   Many, much, a lot.

  Passel ov maids un tha charaban trip ta St Ives
                     Lots of girls on the coach trip to St Ives.

Penny liggen   Hard up for money. Out of pocket.

Pilf/Pilth   Fluff under the bed or on the carpet. Dust.

Pisky   Pixie.

  Pisky led   Led astray without reason.

  Pisky ridden   Someone who has a lot of bad luck or minor accidents.

Planching   A wood or plank floor. *Plynken* is Kernewek for plank.

Plentay of shailt Plenty of sail.

Poor   Tainted, bad.

Propur   Proper, satisfactory, well done.

  Et waas a propur job
                     It was a job well done.

Purdy   Good, as in 'I'm feeling good'.

Purdy!   Exclamation of approval. Well done, great.

Put ome   To shut, close.

  Faathur eeve tha caat owt n put ome tha door
                     Father throw the cat out and shut the door.

Quail   To wither.

Queal/Quill   Pen.

Queck sticks/Quick sticks
Soon done.

Ee maade queck sticks ov washun tha windurs
He soon washed the windows.

Rale   Real.

Raunish   Ravenous.

I'm raunish, I cud ate tha oss and chaase tha drivur
I'm ravenous, I could eat the horse and chase the driver.

Ruff es raats   Rough as rats, not feeling too good.

Runner   A rolled up cloth put behind the door to stop draughts.

Scat   Break. Can also refer to a beat in music.

Tha band waas thray scats behind
The band was three beats behind.

Screech like a whitnik
To cry like a fool.

Schemey   To plan, to use one's head, to contrive.

Those that caan't schemey must lowster
Those that can't plan must labour.

Shrub   To rob.

Shrub tha nest   To rob a bird's nest of eggs.

Shurds   Broken pieces of glass, china or pottery.

Skeet   To clean with water. In some areas a cup of skeet means a cup of tea.

Sleep   Mildew.

Tha boots en tha spence ave gone ta sleep
The boots in the cupboard under the stairs have gone mildewed.

Slock   To entice.

Doan't eeve tha kiddly owt, yew'll slock tha raats
Don't throw the milky sops out, it will entice rats.

Smeech   Smell caused by something burning in the oven.

Soas   Friend, mate, colleague.

Stagged   Covered in mud.

Stagged owt   Having loads of work.

Stank   Long walk. From the Cornish *stankya*. *Stank* in Cornish means heavy tread.

Stram   To walk with purpose.

Stream   To wash, rinse.

  I'm gwain ta stream tha dabber'd clothes
                   I'm going to wash the muddy clothes.

Tacker   Small child, toddler.

Taake et up   Resent it.

  Doan't saay nuthun ta un cos ee da taake et up sum then awful
                   Don't say anything to him because he resents it.

Tend to   To look after, wait upon.

Terrify   To annoy.

  Stop terrifying tha budgie
                   Stop annoying the budgerigar.

Tews n wans   Favourites.

  Tha taychur do ave es tews n wans
                   The teacher does have his favourites.

Tonguetabbis   Chatterbox.

To wance   At once.

Truck   Nonsense.

  Yew doan't want ta ave no truck weth ee
                   You don't want to take any nonsense from him.

Turn ee ta doors Kicked out, shown the door.

Twadn me   It wasn't me.

Urge   To retch or strain in vomiting.

Ussel   Hustle.

  Ussel an bussel ov everay-daay livun
                   Hustle and bustle of everday living.

Vamp   To augment a half empty cup.

Vennegar ill   (Looking) bad tempered.

Vexed   Annoyed.

Vicker   Vicar.

Villidge   Village.

Wat-ee-me-call'd? What's his name?

Wisht Thin, sickly, miserable, sad looking. This saying came about from the belief that someone with supernatural power wished another person ill.

Bessie's lukun wisht Bessie's looking ill.

Woss on? What's on?

Yarn Talk.

Yew/Yiew/Yoo You.

Zackly Exactly, spot on, right, precise.

'Diew yew want et dun zackly?' 'Wull near nuff.' 'Knaw zackly wat yew mane.'
'Do you want it done precisely?' 'Well near enough.' 'I know exactly what you mean.'

Zam-zoodled Half cooked, half baked – or sometimes the opposite, over cooked, over baked.

Zawn A fissure in a cliff. *Saun* means cranny or fissure in Kernewek.

Zound Faint, swoon.

Anemaals, Burds an Ensexs

With Cornwall being such a rural area, it was natural for many animals, birds and insects to have their own dialect names. Some of these are the same in both dialect and the Cornish language. Names varied from area to area; this glossary is a list of some of the more common dialect words.

Airy mouse/Flitter mouse Bat.

Annet Kittiwake.

Applebird Chaffinch.

Bucpicker/Hoop Bullfinch.

Bullhorn/Jan jeak Snail.

Chet Kitten.

Chipper Crossbill.

Chiff-chaff   Chaffinch.
Chow, Chuff   Chough.
Corniwillen   Lapwing.
Daddy Longlegs/Tommy Tailor
    Crane fly.
Dishwasher   Wagtail.
Emmet/Muryan   Ant, *Muryon* is Kernewek for ant.
  Yew caant move fur emmets en St Ives.
    The word emmet is also used for tourists.
Fairy   Weasel.
Fitcher   Polecat or ferret.
Flay   Flea.
Fuzzy pig/Hedgyboard
    Hedgehog.
God's cow   Ladybird.
Grammersow/Zowbugs/Sowpigs
    Woodlouse.
Gray/Grey   Badger.
Hackmale   Blue tit.
Hibet/Padger paw/Padgy paw
    Newt, lizard. Padgy paw etc is derived from *peswar paw*, the Kernewek for newt and lizard. *Peswar paw* literally means four feet.
Hornywink   Toad.
Horse adder/Noss adder
    Dragon fly.
Jannerd/Jennard/Winnard
    Redwing.
King   Donkey.
Knot cow   A cow without horns, having a knot or knob on the top of its head instead.
Lagyar   Moorhen. *Lagyar* is also the name in Kernewek.
Liant   Lion.
Marlion   Merlin.

Moyle	Mule.
Oliphant	Elephant.
Quilkin/Wilky	Frog. From Kernewek *quylkyn*.
Ranny	Wren.
Ruddock/Rabbin	Robin redbreast. Ruddock comes from the Kernewek word *rudhak*.
Soyle	Seal.
Shaip	Sheep.
Tagworm	Earthworm.
Tern	Bittern.
Veer	A young suckling pig.
Want	Mole.
Whitneck	Weasel.
Widden	Small pig.
Winnard	Redwing (a winter migrant).

Lukun lik a winnard
Looking cold and woebegone.

The most famous bird in Cornwall is the chough. It is the emblem of Cornwall and stands proud on the coat of arms. Folklore links the chough to the legend of King Arthur. Many believe that the king did not die that day in battle, instead his spirit was incarnated in the chough.

Once these birds were plentiful, but slowly they disappeared until the last remaining chough died in 1973. In 2001 three choughs returned. These could have returned from Wales, Ireland or Brittany, and took up residence in their homeland. In 2002 these choughs built a nest and bred in Cornwall for the first time in fifty years.

The following poem, which won the Cornish Gorsedd prize for dialect verse in 2002, tells the story of the return of the Cornish chough, the secrecy that surrounded the event, the attempt by egg thieves to rob the nest and the triumphant hatching of the chicks. I think it demonstrates how current news can still be conveyed poetically in dialect.

Gud News

1. *Mygar,*
   tha wind blaw'd
   em en. Thray obem.
   Doan't saay bee or bow.

2. *Chuffs,*
   stoall theer nest
   fram ovur tha watur.
   Doan't tull a saul.

3. *Propur,*
   makun tha moast
   ov cummun ome.
   Kape et ta yerself.

4. *Ansum,*
   hen's clucky, sittun
   es tight es a dam.
   Saay nuthun.

5. *Ell-up,*
   sum party tri'd
   ta shrub tha nest.
   Doan't coose bout et.

6. *Purdy,*
   tha eggs es bealed
   Arfurr es back.
   Tull tha werld.

Down un tha Farm

In addition to the main industries – mining, fishing, china clay and tourism – of past and present Cornwall, farming has always been a vital part of Cornish life.

Farming consists of dairy, pig and sheep farms and general farms with a bit of everything. There are farms that are a part of the flower-growing industry and others that devote part of their land to the broccoli or potato trade.

Conversation in farming families, where the land has been handed down for generations, is still rich in dialect. For example, *'Ays cut n carr'd en putt en a ay rick'*, and *'Gwain lik a oss en a arra.'*

Farming also has many customs; one of the most popular of these, revived by the Old Cornwall Movement, is *Crying The Neck*. This is an end of harvest ceremony. The last stand of wheat is cut (sometimes by the oldest cutter) shaped into a hen's head and neck (*Pen Yar* in Cornish) and held aloft with these cries and responses:

The Cutter: I have'n! I have'n! I have'n!
The Others: What have ee? What have ee? What have ee?
The Cutter: A Neck! A Neck! A Neck!

This custom can be repeated in Kernewek (Cornish language):

An Tregher: Yma genef! Yma genef! Yma genef!
An Ra-crel: Pandr'us genes? Pandr'us genes? Pandr'us genes?
An Tregher: Pen Yar! Pen Yar! Pen Yar!
An Ra-crel: Houra! Houra! Houra!

The neck afterwards may be made into a miniature sheaf or fashioned into a corn dolly and carried home or to a church for a special service.

Altur tha pigs	To castrate pigs.
Ardar	Plough. *Ardar* comes from Kernewek, meaning plough.
Arrish/Arish	A cornfield after the corn is cut.
Balch	A stout bit of rope or cord.
Beal	Bill.
Tha eggs es beal'd	When a chick's bill pokes through a hatching egg.
Bern/Burn	A bundle, as of ferns, hay, sticks, tied round with straw or corn.
Biddicks	Long bladed turf digger.
Bolt	A stone covered drain.
Bowgie/Bowjy	From the Kernewek word *bowjy* for a sheep or cattle house.
Butt	A two wheeled cart.
Cawed	A sheep affected with the rot.
Cazier	A sieve for sifting grain.
Chall	A cattle house.
Chip	The foot of a plough.
Chisle	To tear up ground cleanly.
Cloam egg	An earthenware egg, given to hens to encourage them to lay.
Clucky hen	A broody hen.
Cob	A mixture of coarse brown clayey earth and straw used for building cob walls.
Cornish hair	Rough wool of ancient sheep.
Croft	Rough grazing land, enclosed from the moor, but not cultivated.

Cues	Ox shoes.
Drashun	Thrashing corn.
Drashur	A thrasher of corn.
Dung	Manure.
Eaver	Rye grass.
Eval/Evil/Yule	Four or five pronged manure fork.
Farmun	Farming.
Fleams	Steel blades hammered into an animal's vein in order to bleed the sickness of the animal or to weaken it prior to slaughter.
Fore-ends/Headlands	Strips of land left unploughed and later ploughed at right angles.
Gaver	Goat. *Gaver* is Kernewek for goat. *Gaverhale* is its bleating sound.
Glaws/Gloas/Gloz	Dried cowdung collected to be used for fuel (*gloas* in Kernewek).
Gone ta lie	Corn battered down by weather.
Gurry	Hand wheelbarrow.
Harve/Arra	Harrow.
Ibble	Small pile of corn.
Iles	Awns or beards of barley.

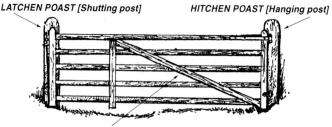

LATCHEN POAST [Shutting post]   HITCHEN POAST [Hanging post]

BRAACE [Brace – diagonal bar]

According to a General View of the Agriculture of the County of Cornwall, on 19th March 1810, this quote relates to the gate illustrated: 'The present high price of timber, a five barred gate seven feet and a half by four feet with one coat of paint cost 15 shillings.'

Kersey wave Stone laid in a herringbone pattern in a hedge.

Kitty bags Pieces of sack tied around the trouser legs for protection.

Lease cattle/cow Cattle not fattened. Milkless cows.

Mabyer Pullet (from the Cornish word *mabyar*, meaning young fowl).

Mait tha pigs Feed the pigs.

Mo Pig. Fair mo – pig fair (*Mogh* is Kernewek for pigs or swine).

Mow A pile of sheaves of corn in a field. *Hand mows* have about 50-60 sheaves, *knee mows*, built by climbing on top, have about 100 sheaves.

Mick owt To clean out cowsheds or stables.

Munger/Mungar Straw horse collar.

Patch hook Bill hook.

Pook/Pouk Pile of hay or turfs.

Regratur One who buys up butter, eggs from a farmer to sell on.

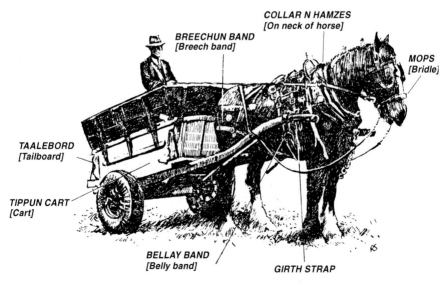

This drawing of a farm cart and horse in harness, is based on a photograph taken at a ploughing match during the 1920s. Rubber tyres were beginning to replace the traditional cart wheels about this time.

OALL RITE ME ANSUM!

HAYMAKING c1900

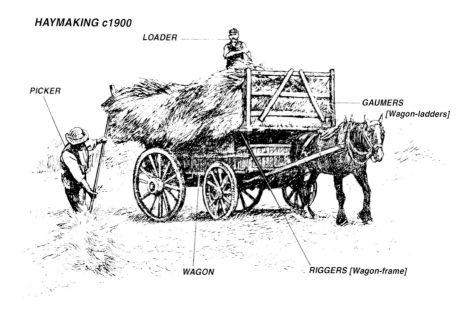

LOADER

PICKER

GAUMERS
[Wagon-ladders]

WAGON

RIGGERS [Wagon-frame]

BANKING PLOUGH (A BANKER)

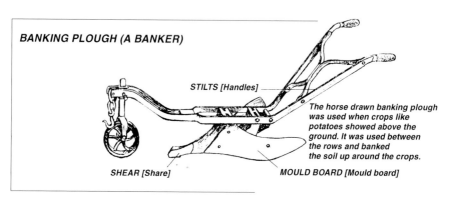

STILTS [Handles]

The horse drawn banking plough was used when crops like potatoes showed above the ground. It was used between the rows and banked the soil up around the crops.

SHEAR [Share]

MOULD BOARD [Mould board]

HEDGING TOOLS

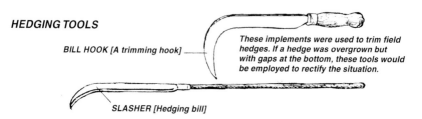

BILL HOOK [A trimming hook]

These implements were used to trim field hedges. If a hedge was overgrown but with gaps at the bottom, these tools would be employed to rectify the situation.

SLASHER [Hedging bill]

Scaade/Scoad/Skid dung
    To spread manure in the fields.

Shock   A pile of sheaves (6 to 8 sheaves) of corn.

Sickle   In the 18th century the sickle, with its curved blade and short handle, was the most common harvest implement in Cornwall.

Snead/Snyd   The handle of a scythe.

Stand ta work   Farm labourer.

Tallet   A stable loft. *Talyk* is loft in Kernewek.

Teel   To plant.

That n tuthur   The traditional method, in Cornwall, of distinguishing between the near horse and the far horse when they are working side by side.

Town plaace   A farmyard with its outbuildings.

Veer   Farrow.

Weaning bridle   A harness made of leather with metal spikes used to prevent calves sucking their mothers.

Winky   To make straw ropes.

Yaffer   Heifer.

Yafful   A handful of hay.

Fishun

The fishing industry in Cornwall is probably no less ancient than mining. There were four main types of fishing – seining, drifting, long lining and crabbing.

Seining was the name of the inshore fishing for pilchards. Watch was kept for the reddish brown streak below the surface of the sea, by men known as huers, who were stationed on the clifftops. The huts they watched from, known as huers' huts, can still be seen today in St Ives and Newquay.

As soon as a shoal of fish was sighted the huers would shout '*Hevva!*', which is Cornish for a shoal of fish. A quote from the *Western Morning News* of 14 October 1881 emphasises the spotting of a shoal. *Hevva! The welcome sound of hevva was heard at St Ives yesterday, and the boats on the lookout for pilchards were instantly on the alert.*

Once the huer had directed the boats into position they would shoot the seine.

The great net was pulled around in a large circle and the mass of fish was drawn in towards the beach. In 1834 it was reported that on one occasion thirty million pilchards were caught by seining in one hour.

As soon as the fish were caught they were rushed to the fish cellars for *bulking* – storage in piles with alternate layers of salt. After being in bulk for a few weeks the pilchards were transferred to barrels, where they were pressed by large stones to extract their oil.

The fishing industry today in Cornwall moves with the times and although the work is somewhat different the fishermen are still very proud of their industry and are doing their utmost to make sure it survives for the next generation of Cornish fishermen.

It is also interesting to note that among the many characters in the history of fishing two fishwives will always be remembered: the 18th century's Dolly Pentreath from Mousehole, of course, who is thought to have been the last speaker of Cornish, and Mary Kelynack, who at the age of 84 walked to London from Newlyn to see the Great Exhibition of 1851.

The following glossary of fishing lists many of the different words for fish and other dialect words and phrases that were common in the industry:

Angelmaine   Monkfish.

Barble   A fisherman's apron made of oilskin, worn when hauling nets.

Beefy	A word used to describe the mending of the fish nets.
Bestin et	Going to sea hoping the weather will improve.
Boulter	A long fishing line with short branches and lots of hooks.
Bulking	Bulking of pilchards was mostly carried out by women. The fish were built into a solid rectangular block, layers of fish being alternated with layers of salt.
Busker	A fisherman who dares all types of weather – an out and out fisherman.
Bussa/Buzza	Large earthenware pot used to salt pilchards in.
Caper-longer	Razor shell fish.
Chad	A young bream.
Cowal/Cowel/Cowle	
	Cowel is a Kernewek word for the fish basket carried on the back.
Cowl	A fish bladder.
Cran	A cran of herrings is 800 herrings.
Dippers	In the catching of pilchards, boats used for the purpose of conveying fish from the net to the shore were known as dippers.

Dogga	Dogfish.
Driving nets	Nets drawn after the boats, fastened only at one end. Fish are caught in the net mesh as they try to pass through.
Drover	The name for a fishing boat used to catch fish with a driving net.
Fairmaids	Cured pilchards, prepared for a market overseas.
Fish fag	Wife of a fisherman.
Frock	Standard wear for a fisherman.
Gaver	Crayfish.
Huer	A watchman employed to look for shoals of fish.
Jousting/Fish jousting/Jowsting	
	Hawking fish, a job usually done by a fishwife.
Kibling	Stealing fish.
Lave tha end go	To undo the mooring rope.
Long nose	Sea pike.
Maglan	Fish ladle.
Meas	A quantity of herrings – 505 herrings.
Morgy/Murgy	The same word *morgy* is in Kernewek and it is the name for a sea dog – spotted dogfish.
Ore weed	Seaweed.
Queen Mackerel	Large fish that heads a shoal of mackerel.
Scad	Mackerel.
Scule/Scool/Skule	Shoal of fish.
Seine boats	Three boats were usually used in seining for pilchards, two large boats and one small one. The large boats were distinguished with the names *seine boat* and *follower* and the small one was known as the *lurker*. Each large boat contained seven men; the master seiner, one other man and two boys were in the small one.
Stoiting	Describes the leaping of a shoal of fish.
Tucking	A job in seining when the net is gradually drawn together.
Train oil	Oil pressed from pilchards.
Treag/Trig	Small shellfish like limpets and periwinkles.

Food n Drenk

Bak'd figgie pudden
A pudding made from flour, suet, mixed fruit and breadcrumbs.

Chuck   Pasty meat.

Cornish crame   Home-made Cornish cream is delicious. It is made by bringing a saucepan of milk to just below boiling temperature, then carefully putting it to one side overnight, next morning skimming off the cream from the top and putting it into a separate dish.

Cornish crame tay   Scones, jam and cream. Join in the great debate – should the jam or the cream go on the scone first?

Crib/Crouse   Break for a snack or meal.

Hevve caake   Heavy cake – an inch thick, flat, rectangular currant cake baked on a sheet.

Hog's pudden   Most butchers keep their hog's pudding recipes secret. This delicacy can be eaten hot or cold. A home-made hog's pudding consists of 1 lb lean minced pork, ½ lb of breadcrumbs moistened with an egg, and salt, pepper and mixed herbs to taste, all boiled for three hours inside a pigskin.

Jammy maw   Jam spread on a slice of bread.

Leeky pie   Leek pie.

Muggety pie   Intestines of a pig cut up and covered with onions, baked for about an hour in a greased dish.

Oggie   Pasty.

Ole Cornish pie   Parsley pie.

Pastay	Yew'll enjoy findun thus wan owt fer yerself me ansum.
Raw fry	Swede, potatoes and bacon dish.
Saffern caake	Fruit cake that uses saffron to colour it. In the late 1950s saffron used to cost 1/6d a dram and it was the dearest item in a grocery shop, as in a pound per pound, hence the dialect expression, *Es dear es saffern.*
Seedy caake	Cake with caraway seeds.
Skirt	Pasty meat.
Star-gazy pie	Pilchards, mackerel or herrings can be used; the pie has slits in the top so the heads of the fish poke through and star gaze.
Tattay	Potato.
Tay	Tea.
Suggery tay	Tea with sugar is a traditional drink with a pasty.
Tay-trate-bun	Large saffron bun given to children on outings and feasts known as tea treats.
Thundur n lightnun	
	A slab of home-made white bread soaked in black treacle, then covered in Cornish clotted cream. *Ansum,* especially when eaten after a bacon and egg breakfast.
Turmut	Swede.
Under roast	Steak and onions with potatoes on top cooked in the oven.

Dreckly

Everyone that visits or comes to live in Cornwall remarks on the slower pace of life.

Dreckly	Could be a lot longer than later.
I'll do it dreckly	I'll do it . . . Some people think dreckly is like manyana, which means tomorrow, but in Cornwall dreckly is more like the day after – the day after tomorrow. This should explain everything. If not, read on:

Ashes caat   A person or an animal that likes being near to the fire.

Cummen ta cum like tha ole wommen's buttar
              Nearly finished.

Ee edden worth es salt
              Lazy person.

Es et thet time oall ridy?
              Is it that time already?

Fortay winks   A short nap.

I fergot meself   I went to sleep.

I'll jus ave five minnuts
              Break from work.

Sha's ta slaw ta carray cold denner
              She's too slow to carry cold dinner (ie can't do a simple job
              in a given time).

Time fer a touch pipe
              A smoke break.

Passun tha time ov daay

Commes en   Come in (inviting someone into your home).

Luke-un sum fitty You're looking good.

My/Me ansum, luvver, burd, boay
              All terms of endearment.

Oall rite my/me ansum?
              Are you all right my friend?

Ow ee do-un? How are you?

Plaise If you please.

Opun tha dore if yew plaise
Open the door please.

Plaise? Pardon? Please repeat.

Rite on All right, fine. Two people who know one another may pass each other and both just say 'right on' as a greeting.

See yew dreckly See you soon; dreckly can mean sometime in the future.

Woss un en pard? What's on then partner? What's on then my friend?

Yewr and es bleedun
Greeting for someone eating a pasty. The gravy is running over your hand.

Yo/Yew Either of these words can be shouted as a greeting, especially by a boisterous person.

Cullurs

Black n white maakes graay.
Rid n yalla maakes oringe.
Yalla n blaw maakes graain.
Rid n blaw maakes purpull.
Rid n black }
Rid n graain } oall maake broawn.
Rid, blaw n yalla }
Rid, black, wite, blaw, yalla n graain maake ell ov ah mess!
Black n goald es tha cullurs ov tha Cornish rugby team.

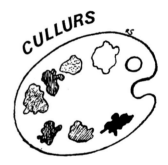

Colours (English) – *Lywyow* **(Kernewek)**
Black – *Du*, Blue – *Glas*, Brown – *Gell*, Gold – *Owr*, Green – *Gwer*, Grey – *Los*, Purple – *Purpur*, Red – *Ruth*, White – *Gwyn*, Yellow – *Melen*.

Tha Human Bodee

Ashes   Exact likeness.

Ee's tha ashes ov es faathur
He's the exact likeness of his father.

Baw legged   Bow legged.

Brackety   Freckled.

Caage ov bones   A thin person.

Chacks   Cheeks.

Chamy   A toothless person.

Clicky   Left handed. From the Kernewek *cledhek*.

Cribbage faace   A thin wrinkled face.

Dull   Hard of hearing.

Fishog/Fissog   Face. Fishog may have been derived from the word physiognomy, which is the art of judging character by the contours of the face.

Go by tha ground   A short person.

Gwain ome fast   Dying.

Haaf bak'd   Slightly lacking.

Put en weth tha bred n tuke owt weth tha caakes
Put in with the bread and taken out with the cakes.

Lug holes   Ears.

Nawse   Nose.

Nuddock   Head.

Pin bone   The hip.

Pin tailed   A person with narrow hips.

Podge/Stuggy   A short, fat person.

Quailaway   Stye on the eye.

Scruff   A scruff can mean an untidy person.

Snob   Nasal secretion.

Tummuls   Large or fat stomach.

Uzzle	Adam's apple.
Vlicker up	To blush.

Human Car-rack-ter-es-tiks

Balk up tha wind To belch, to bring up wind.

Begritch sumwan Begrudge someone.

Belong ta do tha washun Mondaays
Belong is an expression of habit, as in someone always doing the washing on Mondays.

Brave Well, fit.

Buster Buster describes someone full of fun and mischief.

Cab-and'd Awkward.

Catch en tha voice
A speech impediment.

Comfortable If someone is 'comfortable' they are easy to get along with.

Deep as Dolcoath Secretive – Dolcoath is the deepest mine in Cornwall.
  Ees es deep es Dolcoath

Doxy maid A petite young female.

Fitty Proper.
  Ee doaes a fitty job
He does a job properly.

Fly by nite Someone who is irresponsible.

Givish Generous.
  Sha's rite givish She's very generous.

Gwain un quietly A little deceptive – it can mean that someone is doing very nicely.

Lipsy Someone who talks with a lisp.

Oogly/Ugly Cross, bad tempered.
  Missus waas as oogly es sin cos I waas laate fur my denner
The wife was very cross because I was late for my dinner.

Ome from ome Very familiar with everything.

Over tha moon In good spirits.

Puff'd up	Pompous.
Pushie	Ambitious, someone who gets on by any means.
Ee's sum pushie	
Run word	To go back on one's word.
Sludge tha feet	To drag the feet.
Snotty	Snobbish. Someone who thinks they are above their station in life.
Strate es a die	Honest, straighforward and reliable.
Takun leave ov theer senses	
	Someone doing something extremely foolish.
Taisy/Teasy	Bad tempered. From *tesek*.
Missus es taisy es a adder, sha's reallay snakey	
	The wife is as bad tempered as a disturbed snake.
Tongue tied	Too shy to speak.

Tha Kiddleywink (The Pub)

Kiddleywink was the name for unlicensed beer shops; some may have had a semi licence. Regular customers used to wink at the kettle (kiddle) for brandy or moonshine. Later there were pubs that took the name Kiddley.

Anker	A small cask or keg used for brandy.
Baccca/Backey	Tobacco.
Drunk es a mattruss	
	Flat out with drink.
Drunk es a Piraneer	
	St Piran the patron saint of Cornwall was known to like a drink.
Es piss'd es a newt	
	Country phrase describing a drunk.
Gwain ta straain tha tatties	
	Going to the toilet.
Lapshipa	Alcoholic drink.

Mahogany/Black Star gin n trikle
Gin sweetened with treacle.

Prilled   Half drunk.

Sampson   A drink of cider, brandy and a little water, with sugar.

Sampson weth es hair un
Made with a double brandy.

Slewed/Tadly-oodly
Tipsy.

Swipes   A thin small alcoholic drink.

Tom Toddy   A game in which each person in succession has to drink a
                               glass of beer or spirits, on the top of which a piece of burning
                               candle has been put, whilst the others sing:
                               Tom Toddy es coom hoam, coom hoam,
                                 Tom Toddy es coom hoam,
                               Weth es eyes burnt, and es nawse burnt
                               and es eyelids burnt,
                                 Tom Toddy es coom hoam ...

Tot   Dram or nip of spirit.

Traade   General term for alcoholic liquor.

Wullee ave a drop ov moonshine?
Will you have a drop of smuggled brandy?

In *Cornwall and its People*, A.K. Hamilton Jenkins writes about a signboard above
the door of the Tinners' Arms at St Hilary in the 19th century.

> *Come all good Cornish boys, walk in,*
> *Here's to brandy, rum and shrub and gin,*
> *You can't do less than drink success*
> *To Copper, Fish and Tin.*

'You say you consider the defendant was not drunk.
Will you tell the magistrate when you consider a man
is drunk.'
  'Wael wan ee taakes es murthur fur es faathur.'
(*Cornish Magazine 1989*).

The Cornish have always been noted for their fine voices; many a night ends in a traditional Cornish pub with a good singsong. Great favourites like *Trelawney*, *Goin Up Camborne Hill*, *Cornwall Forever*, *Away Down To Lamorna*, *The White Rose*, *Hail To The Homeland* and *Little Liza* can be heard.

'Aftur a skin-full ov beer, tis ansum, yew've nevur eard nuthun lik et.'

Minun (above and below grass)

Cornwall has always been known for its mining wealth, and the landscape still reminds us of miners who went in search of copper, tin, lead, zinc, iron and rarer metals. The history of mining goes back into the mists of time; it is said the Phoenicians came to Cornish shores to barter for crudely smelted tin. Another story is how Joseph of Arimathea came here with a young Jesus to trade for tin.

Early tin streaming was widespread in the county. However, it is certain that true lode mining did not commence until the Middle Ages. Tin was the main metal mined until about 1700; then gradually copper mining came into its own and reached its peak by 1860.

There are excellent books that cover the history of mining up to the closures of the 20th century and are worth reading.

Superstitions and tales from miners lend themseves nicely to dialect.

Cornish miner Mike Osman was once asked where he worked. 'Crofty,' Mike answered. '*Ess, I thawt so, white faace an rusty ands*,' was the reply.

It wasn't uncommon for a miner to leave home before daybreak and return in the dark. *En oaldun daays a roostur lock'd en a cubbard serv'd es a clock sence ee crow'd wen et waas time ta git up.*

Miners were very superstitious. *Ef thay saw a snail un tha waay ta tha bal thay'd drop a bit ov tallow fram theer candull by tha side obem else thay'd ave bad luck.*

Wen thay lef ome fer work thay nevur go back even ef thay ad fergot sumtheng. This superstition resulted in tragedy for two miners that ignored it. One man who forgot to say goodnight to his mates in the pub before he went to work went back to do so and was killed later that night in the shaft. Another man who returned home to get his towel was killed in the Levant disaster.

Naw whislun. To whistle underground might upset *tha knockers* (the little people) and result in bad luck. To appease *tha knockers et crouse time miners wud leave a didjan* (a morsel of food or a corner of pasty).

Miners liked good boots for work – they were known as *gud understanduns*. Many enjoyed a smoke underground and this was known as a *touch pipe*. They also observed the custom of first down/first up. This was known as *catch yer turn*.

Adventurers	Those who have shares in a mine.
Audit/Odit	Adit.
Banjo	A small shovel.
Bal	Mine. The word is the same in Kernewek and dialect.
Black tin	Tin ore fit for the smelting or blowing house.
Blawing house	A place for melting tin.
Cap'n	Captain. The man who was in charge of the operations at a mine.
Cobbing	Breaking the ore with hammers.
Coffin	Old workings open to the surface mostly made by *oald men*, the name for ancient workers.
Cores	Mining term for shifts. Long ago miners worked six-hour shifts.

Vorenoon core (6 am – noon); Avnoon core (noon – 6 pm);
          Furst core (6 pm – midnight); Last core (midnight – 6 am)
          In the 1970s at Crofty mine there were three shifts, 7 am – 3 pm; 3 pm – 11 pm and 11 pm – 7 am.

Dag   A mining axe.

Dam   A constructed barrier shutting out or impounding water.

Dead ground   Part of the lode without ore.

Dredgy ore   Inferior metal.

Injun stack   Lofty chimney of an engine house.

Fang   Niche cut out in an adit side.

Fanging   Earnings.

    Ow much ave yew fanged thus month?
          How much have you earned this month?

Filchering   When the drill jammed in a crack in the rock.

Footway/Ladderway/Ladder road
          Ladders for descending and ascending in a mine.

Gad   A wedge-shaped tool used to split rock.

Gook	A bonnet worn by mine maidens.
Grass	The mine's surface.
Gunnis	An area where the lode has been worked; the empty space is known as a gunnis.
Hole to grass	Working a vein of metal to the surface.
Hutch work	Small ore washed by a sieve.
Idle	When mine work has stopped or the mine has been abandoned.
Jews house	A smelting place for tin.
Jigging	Separating the ore with a griddle.
Just alive	When there is a very small amount of ore in the stone.
Kibble	An iron mine bucket that goes up and down in a shaft.
Kitting	Stealing ore.
Ta kit	To steal ore.
Knack'd bal	A mine that is no longer working.
Launders	Guttering or tubes used for the conveyance of water.
Learys	Remains of very old mining and stream workings carried out by ancient miners.
Lode	A vein that produces any type of metallic ore.
Man injun	This widely used engine, which was first introduced around 1830 at Tresavean mine, lowered mine workers underground and lifted them up again.
More	A large quantity of ore in a certain part of a load is known as a more of tin.
Nog/Nay	Support for the mine roof.
Oald men	This does not mean aged men but refers to ancient mine workers from long ago.
Ooze	Hose.
Peeker an a poker	Names given to chisels for cutting hitches in a rock down at Geevor mine.
Pillar	Ground left to support the roof or wall in a mine.
Prospecting	Sinking trial holes in search of a lode.
Pot ground/Pot granite	
	Rotten granite, not necessarily cracked, loose or dangerous.

GLOSSARY

Pride ov tha countray
When ore is found in great abundance and very rich near the surface it is said to be the pride of the country.

Queer A queer bit of ground – a square of land.

Rack rag frame An inclining frame used to wash and separate ores.

Raffain Ore of no real value.

Sampling Testing the quality of mine ores.

Schale of earth Earth slide in an excavation.

Seam A load.

Skove A rich load, pure and clean.
Tis oall skove

Slimes Finest crushed ore.

Smelting house Building where ore is reduced to pure metal by fire.

Stamp Machine used to crush ore.

Stope A corruption of the word step, to describe how the lode is removed in benches or steps. Correctly, an area where the lode is *being worked* is a stope. Where the lode *has been worked* and is now finished, the empty space is called a gunnis.

Stull Support timber.

Tributer A miner whose pay is a proportion of the value of ore raised (a tribute).

Tull Old name for a miner's hat.

Tutwork Work that earns according to the amount of labour; payments for driving, sinking at a price per fathom. This can also be the price for a job.

Underline shaft A diagonal shaft on the lode course.

Vamping Vamping is a layer of broken dirt on the floor of a drive above the bedrock.

Vugh/Vugg/Vogle A cavity.

Wheal Common word for mine, usually used as a prefix to the name of most mines, eg Wheal Jane.

Whim/Whym Kernewek name for the machine for raising ore, worked by either steam, horse or water.

| Zyghyr | When a slow stream of water issues through a cranny it is said to zygher or sigger. |

Owse an Ome

Bed tye	Feather mattress.
Bussa	Earthenware pot.
Caddle	To do housework in an untidy manner.
Cherks	Cinders from a coal fire.
Chill	A small earthenware lamp used when they burned train oil (the oil fried out of the gut of pilchards). A rush with its skin peeled off was used for a wick.
Chimbly	Chimney.

Tha chimbly es smaukun braave
The chimney is smoking a lot.

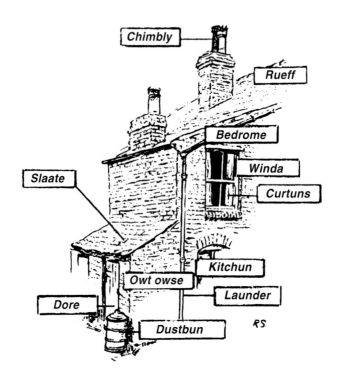

Cloam	Dishes.
Cloam oven	An earthenware oven built into a hearth. A fire was lit inside the oven and then the oven was cleaned out. Food was cooked into the slow diminishing heat.
Drang	A narrow passage or lane between walls.
Durns	The frame of a door.
Flasket	A clothes basket.
Flies	Hands on a clock.
Imbleach	Unbleached linen.
Launder	Guttering.
Planchum	A wooden planked floor.
Po	A chamber pot.
Beds not maade n poes not emptud	
	This expression was used when one was caught out with unexpected visitors to the home.
Slab	A Cornish range fireplace.
Slush lavitory	Flush toilet.
Spense	Cupboard under the stairs. My mother was afraid of thunder and lightning. When this event happened she would hide from it in the spense.
Timberran hill	The stairs.

Sports

Feer Plaay! Feer Plaay! Maake a Ring . . .

When Cornishmen fought, or cudgelled or wrestled they did so generously, very often for the sake of prowess and without a sign of rancour.

Cudgelling	A game of fencing with stout sticks or cudgels. The man who first brought blood was declared the winner.
Gware wheag yu gware teg. (Sporting motto in Kernewek)	
	Fair play is good play.
Hurling	In olden days hurling was a chief sport in Cornwall. Often parish played against parish. Now in St Columb on Shrove

Tuesday hurling the silver ball is still played, with Townmen versus Countrymen. The goals are two miles apart.

Rugby A very definite Cornish sport with a huge following. In 1991 40,000 plus supporters made their way to Twickenham to support Cornwall in the County Championship.

Lass wan ta lave Cornwall swetch tha lite owt

The 'in' saying was, 'Last one to leave Cornwall switch the light out.'

Wrasslin

Wrasslin goes back a long way. No one is sure of its genesis. Drayton, an old poet, says that at the Battle of Agincourt (1415) the Cornish contingent marched onto the field beneath a banner depicting two wrestlers in a hitch.

Richard Carew wrote in 1602, 'You shall hardly find an assembly of boys in Devon and Cornwall where the most untowardly will not as readily give you a muster of this exercise as you are prone to require it.'

In *The Story of Cornwall*, A.K. Hamilton Jenkin quotes another writer from 1662, 'The Cornish are masters of the art of wrestling and to give a Cornish hug is proverbial.'

In 1885 Walter White in *A Londoner's Walk to the Land's End* describes Cornish wrasslin as 'a fine manly exercise'.

In the history of one of the great and still discussed wrestling matches between Polkinghorne of Cornwall and Cann of Devon, author A. Ivan Rabey describes the sport: 'Cornish wrestlers played without shoes and grasped each other by the short jacket which is always worn. A man could be thrust and hugged and thrown and fallen upon.'

The referees or umpires, called sticklers, led to a great dialect phrase:

Ee's a stickler fur tha rules
> He referees by the rules.

Other dialect terms from Cornish wrasslin are:

Cornish hug	A powerful grip.
Fagot	A wrestler who's agreed not to win. It is said he 'sold his back' and he's contemptuously called *fagot*.
Fauns	A fall.
Glock	A throw.
Scat-un-back	The knock back.
Sprag	Used to break an attack.
Vor eap thraw	Fore hip throw.

Threets n Commans

Ballyrag   To abuse or scold someone.

Doan't saay wat I do, just do wat I saay
> Don't say what I do, just do what I say.

Ga fer et   Go for it.

Geve tha fi-er a poke an pull tha kittle forth tis time fer a cup ov tay
> Put the kettle on, it's time for tea.

I'll clot go ta ee en a minnut
> I'll hit you in a minute.

I'll geve ee a gud collopun
> I'll give you a good thrashing.

I'll geve yew wat fer en a minnut
      I'll sort you out in a minute.

I'll scat ee fram ere ta kingdom cum
      I'll knock you into the next world.

Saay nuthun   Say nothing.

Stop screechun or I'll geve ee sumtheng ta screech fer
      Stop crying or I'll smack you, so that you have something to cry about.

Stop squallun   Stop crying.

Tongue pie   Scolding.

Doan't cross er, sha'll geve ee sum tongue pie
      Don't get on the wrong side of her, she will scold you if you do.

Tha Wethur

Blaw-un a gale   Very windy.

Cabby wethur   Damp, humid weather.

Cauld   Cold.

Cortilly wethur   Foggy or misty weather.

Cumun en dirtay   It will soon rain.

Et's a white werld owtside
      It's covered in snow outside.

Et's entun down   It's raining heavy.

Gluthenning up   Gathering into rain (from the Cornish *gluthenna*).

Hag   Mist.

Lashun down   Raining heavily.

Scat ov frost   A sharp frost.

Skivvy rain   Light misty shower.

Sun crackun tha edges
Very hot and sunny.

Dialect Saayuns Bout Tha Wethur

Smauke gwain up strate, sine ov fine wethur. Smauke gwain ta ground, sine ov rain.
Smoke going up straight, sign of fine weather. Smoke going to ground, sign of rain.

Mist un tha moor, bring sun ta tha door. Mist un tha hill bring waatur ta tha mill
Mist on the moor, bring sun to the door. Mist on the hill bring water to the mill.

Rain avore sebben, cleer avore leben
Rain before seven, clear before eleven.

Fi-er burnun blue sine ov cauld wethur
Fire burning blue sign of cold weather.

Et's rainun; git en tha lew
It's raining; go into shelter.

Cauld es a quilkin   Cold as a frog.

Et wull eithur rain or cum dark fur marnun
A dialect quote about the weather that's guaranteed always to be right.

Cauld nuff fur a walkun stick
A bit of dialect humour.

Tis a Chield's Werld

Act up   To play up. Do something for attention.

  Tha boay es actun up

Begs furst/laast etc
I want to go first/last etc.

Chield   Child.

Es et a boay or a chield?

This question would make sense to a dialect speaker as chield can mean a baby girl.

Clidgy nicey   Sticky sweets.

Dandy   A go-cart made by using pram wheels, steered by the feet or by rope tied to the crossbar of the front wheels and tugged from left to right. Sometimes a crude brake was attached to the side of the dandy and when applied would tip the dandy over with its occupant still on board.

Geve uz a ride en yer dandy

Dog dansun   Disobedient behaviour.

En my sebben   Six years old going on towards seven years of age.

Keet   Kite.

Minching/Miching Playing truant.

Mop an heedy   Hide and seek. Mop is the child that covers its eyes and counts while the others hide.

Naw quarterings, naw alfings, naw pick a daniels

Terms used by boys when they find anything, to avoid dispute.

Rounders   A game of bat and ball somewhat like baseball. There is only one batting place, from which there are three stations to run around before reaching the batting place again. Out is being stumped before reaching a station.

Skeer/Skit/Skitter To skim a stone on water.

St Michaels Mount Penzance

Tay-trate   Tea treat.

Tay-trate weth a saffern bun

A Sunday school would organise a tea treat (sometimes to the seaside) for the children. Each child would be given a large saffron bun.

Thray goals n en A game of football between several players with only one goalkeeper. When a player scores three goals he becomes the goalkeeper.

57

CHAPTER 2

Tha Car Weth Naw Naame

This poem was written and entered in the dialect verse section of the 2002 Gorsedd Kernow Competition with another one of my dialect poems, *Gud News*, which is included here in the *Anemaals, Burds an Ensexs* glossary. I was surprised when the results were announced. I got a joint first with the two entries and received the Kewny Cup. I think the simple dialect rhyme scheme helped make *Tha Car Weth Naw Naame* a winner.

Et waas two-toned, goald 'n' rust,
tha numbur pla-ate stat'd trust.
Naw-body knaw'd fram weer et caame
et waas jus tha car weth naw naame.

A stickur un tha windaw rid, relax –
thus car es saw oald yew doan't need tax.
Weth thus car yew need nevur feer
et wull git ee fram A ta B en sec-cun geer.

Theer nevur es a daay goes by
weth-owt tha oil n watur runnun dry.
Ef yew thenk thet tha ownur's ta blaame,
maake a offur fer tha car weth naw naame.

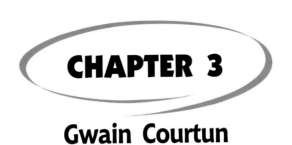

CHAPTER 3

Gwain Courtun

G *wain Courtun* is a favourite short story of mine. So much so that I use the same theme, and the same punch line ending, as my opening number when I do a reading or performance. It never fails to get a warm reception. I hope you enjoy this version of it.

Young Wullie Tresidder waas dun up ta tha nines. Es hair waas eld en a quiff weth brylcrame thet luked lik et wud need a oil chaange en a daay or too. Ee smelt lik a flew-wer shop weth tha vi-let waater ee ad spinkl'd ovur es shart an trousies, while mawthur's back waas turnt.

Young Wullie waas gwain owt courtun weth a maid down un olidaay fram up countray. Es mawthur (Lily Tresidder, yew knaw, Lily Pasca thet waas) wuddun verray ap-pay bout et. Lily reckun'd, sha ad ta chew ovur a morsel weth Young Wullie fer ee wen owt.

'Wullie yewr dun up lik a dog's denner, I waant a word weth ee,' Lily sid ta er boay.

Young Wullie waas daggin ta git gwain, but ee thowt ee ad bettur lissun ta wat mawthur ad ta saay.

'I dos knaw yew es gwain ta see thus maid fram up countray, so I thawt I shud ave a word weth ee, an taint bout tha burds and bays.'

'Caan't et wate til dreckly, Mawthur, I'm oall bayhin now lik a cow's tail,'

Wullie sid, weth a fix'd grin un es faace thet maade en luke lik ee wuddun quite fitty.

'Yew anges on a minnit!' Mawthur snapped, sha sound'd as teasy as a ole adder. 'See gwain courtun weth a up tha countray maid es lie-bull ta git yew led astray.'

'Giss on,' Wullie sid, edge-un tawards tha dore like a crab gwain ta jail.

Mawthur catched old ov es arm, er feers echo'd en er voice. 'Tham up tha countray maids ar lie-bull ta slock ee b'hind tha furse an fer yew cud saay, "Billy Bray caan ee elp me," twud bay taa laate!'

Young Wullie blush'd, es grin spread fram ear ta ear. 'Do yew reckun sha wull?' ee sid an duck'd ta avoid a cloat roun' tha chacks.

'Ere! Ere! Yew caan't saay thengs lik thet en frant ov yewr mawthur,' Missus Tresidder sid. 'Wen I waas a maid an yewr faathur waas gwain owt weth me, we dedden ole ands til we'd bin seeun wan nothur fower sebben months. An I dedden lit im kesse me til we waas courtun propur an ad got me engagemunt ring owt obem.'

Mawthur smilt et tha memoray, than er faace went az black az thundur. Sha gaave Young Wullie a clout un tha nuddock.

'An! And then,' Mawthur snapped, 'do yew knaw wat appen'd!'

'Naw,' sid Young Wullie, gittun riddy ta duck.

'Bayfore we waas mar-red, yew ad ta cum long an bloody spoil thengs! Dedn't yew?'

CHAPTER 4

Tha Oald Womman et Ivy Cottage

Stories about witches are very popular in country folklore. *Tha Oald Womman et Ivy Cottage* is a story line that could come from anywhere in the countryside of Britain. The Cornish setting, the witch's familiars, reference to charms and being written in dialect make it very believable.

Charlay Semmons stramm'd enta thay emptay kiddleywink. Ee wen strate up ta tha bar an gasp'd, 'Beer!' An wait'd weth es mouth abroad.

Tha pint waas ex-purt-lay pult. Tha lan-lurd knaw'd es stuff, ee waas ome fram ome, real propur et es job.

Charlay Semmons, must ave bin es dry es oald boots, ee gaddled alf ov es pint es soon es ee got et, wip'd es mouth un es sleeve, 'Wat do ee knaw bout thet oald womman thet lives en tha cottage gwain owt ov tha village tawurds Trura?' ee ax'd es ost.

'Do ee mane tha oald womman thet lives en Ivy Cottage?' Bill Kemp, lan-lurd ov tha kiddleywink, answur'd by waay ov nothur quest-un ta es onlay custmur.

'Iss, iss tha's tha wan. I feel I knaw er, but I caan't caall er ome,' Charlay rayplied, tryun ta sound a bit vague.

'Queer ole devil.'

'Sha es.' Charlay emptud es glass, un push et tawards tha lan-lurd.

'Saame agin?' Bill Kemp ax'd.

'Iss, iss. Saame agin, I need et.' Charlay rayplied.

'Thay saay sha's a witch!' Bill sid, as ee put tha pint down un tha bar en front ov es customur.

Charlay gasp'd, tuke nothur gaddle, wip'd es mouth agin, an sid en a voice thet didn't seem fitty, 'Giss on?'

'Tis true,' Bill Kemp nodd'd and raypeat'd, 'tis true.'

'A witch,' Charlay sid ta esself, an ran es fingers threw es theck crop ov black hair. Ee luked et es hand, an turn'd et ovur. Wen ee saw Bill Kemp lukun et em ee grizzled, 'A witch.'

'Tha's rite.'

'Giss on!' Charlay sid, wishun ee never ax'd.

Bill Kemp waas warmun ta tha subject. 'Iss, iss, sha es,'' ee continu'd en a con-fid-ent-shall whisper. 'Ded ee see tha toads en er gardun, geat lickurs, an tha ole womman got umteen caats, oall black wans. Naw wandur thay saay sha's a witch.'

'Naw tha's ole wives taales,' Charlay stat'd, thow et mus bay sid ee gone a shaade whitur. 'Thet's naw proof,' ee add'd ta convince esself.

'Sha maakes love po-shuns!' Bill emphasized es point.

'Cods wallop, thet es.'

'I wudden bay ta sure, we've nevur ad a divorce en tha village.'

'Naw. Doan't reckun yew caan put ta much un thet wan. Thet's wat they caall cir-cum-stan-shall,' Charlay ray-sun'd, indee-cate-un ee wantud nothur pint.

Bill Kemp pick'd up tha emptay glass an eld et en front ov Charlay's faace. 'Notice sum theng, do ee?'

'Unlay me emptay glass.'

'Luke et me fingurs!'

'Yer nales es lagg'd,' Charlay grizzl'd. 'Taint propur.'

'Not me nales, me fingurs, naw warts, ad loads ov warts las week I ded. Tha oale womman fram Ivy Cottage charm'd em ovv.' Bill Kemp pult tha pint. 'Tha's tha God's onest trewth thet es, sha ded charm em.' Ee nodd'd. 'Sha caan geve tha evil eye as-wull so thay saay!'

Charlay stared et tha pint. Ee luked like deth warm'd up. Ee ran es fingurs threw es hair agin and then stud'd es hand turnun et ovur an ovur.

'Whiskay, maake et a doub-bull.'

Bill Kemp knawd wen ta kape quiet, ee waas tha perfict lan-lurd. Ee gaave tha glass two gental pushes et tha optic, eld tha glass up ta tha lite, shook es head, an gaave tha optic a queck push ta release nothur drop en ta tha whiskay glass. Ee plaac'd tha glass en front ov Charlay.

'I oall-waays geve gud measure un a doub-bull,' ee sid, nod-dun et tha glass.

Et waas ob-vious-lay appre-sha-atud by Charlay, ee down'd et en wan gaddle, ran es fingurs threw es hair agin an gasp'd. Ee stud up quecklay.

'Sha sid me hair wud fall owt!' he blurt'd, showun Bill Kemp a handful of loose hair.

Tha lan-lurd ray-fill'd tha whiskay glass weth a doub-bull an add'd two drops more fer gud measure. 'Wat ded ee do?' Bill Kemp ax'd.

Charlay Semmons down'd tha whiskay. 'Run ovur wan ov er bloody caats. Kilt et ded.' Ee put tha glass down an turn'd es hands ovur. 'Luke hair es growun un me hands now!' ee exclaim'd.

CHAPTER 5

Wan Fer Sarraw

This short story was inspired by an item of news several years ago, about someone being accidentally shot by a child with a loaded gun. Magpie folklore is an essential ingredient of the tale and I do not believe it really was one magpie for sorrow in this particular case.

Mavis Caddy ad ben tha poast-womman en tha Cornish village ov Penkie fer twen-nee yers. Mavis ad daay-liver'd tha poast ta tha village en-hab-et-tants, owt-lie-yun farms un cot-tages, en oall-sorts ov weth-hur, proud-lay ad-mit-tun sha ad nevur miss'd a daay's wurk en er life.

Oall-tho et waas mid Septembur, et waas ansum weth-hur. Mavis waas stull wearun er sumhur isshue Poast Ovvuss u-ne-form. Tha sun ad shone oall mornun, sha ad oall-moast finush'd er un foot daay-liver-rays an' dedn't feel tired.

Walkun down tha countray rawd ta Orchard Cottage, tha laast daay-liver-ray un er round, Mavis nawticed tha bram-bull strewn hedges waas chuck a block weth black-berrus. Sha maade up er mind ta cum back latur ta pick um.

Tha Munroe famlay mov'd ta Orchard Cottage thray months ago. Mavis wen ta theer ouse wance a month ta daay-liver tha onlay mail thay evur ray-ceiv'd, tha cell-o-faane wrapp'd 'Gun Magazine'.

Mavis lif'd tha lettur box flaap ta be greatud by a rays'd female voice, 'I'm fed up weth yew, an yewr gun mania, et's me or tha guns!'

Wat-evur else waas sid wen unhurd. Tha Gun Magazine fell ta tha floor, tha spring back lettur box flaap snapp'd shut.

Mavis walk'd awaay won-dur-un ef tha handgun law waas beun ignor'd. Sha day-sided et waas nun ov er buznezz. Mavis claws'd tha gerden gaate an nawticed a sol-lit-tary magpie sittun un tha fence.

'Wan fer sarraw,' Mavis sid, spit-tun en tha rawd ta ward ovv bad luck.

Jean Munroe lay un tha bed. Sha breath'd en deep-lay. 'Count ta tin,' sha told erself. Feelun calmur, sha start'd ta thenk lod-gical-lay bout er uzband Bill's obbay ov col-lect-tun handguns.

Oall men need-ded a obbay. Thus waas more then un obbay. Et waas un ob-sess-shun. Sence thay ad moved ta Orchard Cottage, Bill ad ellegally puchaas'd

63

nothur thray handguns fram othur collecturs givun up tha obbay aftur tha tragic Dunblane massacre.

Bill clean'd, load'd an unload'd tha guns um-teen times a daay. Ee waas constant-lay watch'd by Joey, theere sebben yer oald son. Joey waas daggun ta fi-er tha guns. Ee kept askun es faathur ef ee cud old tha guns an fi-er em.

Bill waas ovur tha moon weth es boay's entur-rust. En fairnuss, Bill waas oall-waays careful, Joey onlay handl'd unload'd guns. Bill emfa-sis'd load'd guns waas dan-ger-rus.

Uz a mawthur, Jean believ'd er son onlay associat'd dan-ger-rus weth cross-sun tha rawd wethowt lookun. Sha waas afeer'd, wan daay an ax-ced-dent wud appun.

Uz a wife, Jean felt sha waas balanc'd un a knife edge, tha rows bay-tween er an Bill bout tha guns were becumun more reglar.

Tha row thet mornun ad ben bout a gun left un tha dinun room tay-bull tha nite avore, thenk-ful-lay unload'd. Sha ad foun young Joey play-un weth tha gun wen sha ad taken en es brek-fass.

Jean mede-ate-lay flew unta a raage an con-front'd Bill bout be-un careless. Ee laff'd an sid sha waas ovur re-act-tun, thet waas wen sha threatun ta leb im. Bill dedn't answur, ee jus wen ta collect tha poast ee ad eard beun day-liver'd.

Bill waas flippun thraw tha latest Gun Magazine wen ee cum back enta tha room. Jean rush'd owt ov tha room, slamm'd tha door an stank'd upsteers.

Aving finish'd er dut-tays fer tha village Poast Ovvus, Mavis wen ome. Sha chang'd owt ov er uni-e-form enta cas-u-oall jeans and sweatur.

Mavis ad a jammy maw an a cup ov tay fer er crouse. Soon uz sha ad fenesh'd, sha slipp'd un er walkun shoes an donned an oald poast ovvus beret ta protect er ead fram ovur angun bram-bulls.

Suit-ab-lay attired, an arm'd weth a large jug, sha set ovv ta pick tha black-berrus sha ad seen er-la-ur.

Mavis walk'd ta tha laane leadun ta Orchard Cottage, an start'd ta pick tha moast suc-u-lent black-berrus sha ad evur seen. I've timed thus rite sha thawt, tha black-berrus wur so ripe, thay fell enta er hand wen sha touch'd tham. Mavis oallso knaw'd sha waas pickun obem avore tha 29th of Septembur, wen accordun ta folklore, tha debbel wud spoil tha blackberrus an make tham unsafe ta ate.

Mavis ten-shun ta tha black-berrus waas entur-rupt-tud by a loud raucous caall, tha magpie waas sittun un tha branch ov a nearby tray. Mavis doff'd er beret en salute, nother waay ov wardun ovv bad luck.

'Ovv weth yew, me black n white friend,' sha sid.

Mavis laffed, an tha magpie flew awaay. Me an my sup-per-sti-shuns, sha thawt, ray-turn-un ta tha job en and. Tha ovv dutay poast-womman sang, en a skule plaaygroun' chant, 'Wan fer sarraw . . .'

Jean woke up weth a start, an look'd et tha bedroom clock. Et waas 1.30 en tha avnoon, sha ad ben asleep fer two ours. Sha felt guilty an rush'd downsteers.

Er boay, Joey, waas sittun et tha tay-bull loadun live am-u-nis-shun enta a lethal lookun pistol.

'Joey! Put thet gun down et once. Et's dan-ger-rus!' Jean exclaim'd.

Tha sebben yer oald jump'd. 'I'm not do-un nawthun wrong, Mawthur,' ee whimper'd, uz ee slid tha gun awaay.

'Go owt enta tha gerden an plaay thus min-nit!' es mawthur snapped. 'I want a wurd weth yewr faathur un es own.'

Joey ran owt threw tha patio doors, wethowt a back-ward glance. Bill cum stridun enta tha room an demand'd, 'Woss oall tha row bout, et souns like Lansan jail.'

Fer a momunt Jean waas et a loss fer wurds. En angur sha took er weddun ring ovv an threw et un tha table beside tha a-band-un pistol.

Jean took a deep breath, look'd et er uzband an sid en a calm voice, 'Thet es et, I'm takun Joey ta mawthurs. Tha mar-rage es ovur!'

Sha rush'd upsteers ta pack, follow'd by er uzband protestun et er re-act-shun, avore ee start'd pleadun weth er ta staay.

Joey, hid-dun behin tha Cornish palm en tha gerden, saw an ovurhurd everay-theng. Ee waas won-dur-un wat ta do, wen tha ouse went silent.

Mawthur an Faathur wud be do-un thet sop-pay kissun an makun up, ee reckun'd, run-nun ta plaay un tha swing.

Joey waas swingun highur then ee ad evur dun avore, wen ee saw tha magpie land en tha gardun. Ee slow'd tha swing down by lettun es feet drag un tha groun', es mind raaced tin ta tha dozen.

Magpie, wan fer sarraw. Magpies liked shiny thengs. Mawthur's weddun ring waas shiny. Wan fer sarraw. Joey ran enta tha ouse.

Disturb'd by Joey, tha magpie flew an perch'd un tha gerden gaate, flick'd ets tail an geved a teasy soundun caall.

Joey ran back enta tha gerden clutchun tha pistol. Ee stead'd emself, aim'd an fi-er'd et tha magpie. Tha recoil ov tha pistol scat Joey ta tha groun. Tha magpie screech'd an flew awaay.

Tha bedroom windaw waas throw'd abroad. Bill an Jean shout'd en horror. 'Joey put tha gun down et's dan-ger-rus!'

Tha magpie foun' a saafe plaace ta perch an look'd et Mavis.

'Wan fer sarraw,' Mavis moan'd. Sha waas es white es a goast, an clutchun tha bleedun wound en er leg.

'I'm gwain ta miss wurk fer tha furst time tamorraw,' Mavis sid, bay-fower sha paas'd owt weth tha pain.

CHAPTER 6

Daily Life

Country life is full of anecdotes. I have gathered, preserved and sometimes adapted these glimpses of the everyday happenings that enrich our world.

Enturview

When Missus Laity opun'd er tay room tha 'Wes Britun' newspaapur sent a rayportur owt ta see er fer a enturview.

'Ow oald ar yew Missus Laity?' waas tha furst question tha raypurtur ax'd.

'Thay saay I'll bay nintay en April,' Missus Laity rayplied an' than contenued, but I doan't reckun I am!'

'Oh ow oald ar yew than?' tha rayportur scent'd a storay.

'Nintay un March sexth,' Missus Laity sid. 'See I'll bay ovur nintay en April.'

Football Raysult

'Tha local darby football raysult waas St Ives nil – Carbis Bay nil,' Decky Bray raymark'd.

'Dost ee knaw wat tha score waas et aff time?' Missus Laity ax'd.

Furst Girlfren

Cousin Michael waas tryun ta kesse es furst girlfren en tha ketchun, an sha kept backun awaay fram em. Michael's faathur caam enta tha room, an ee sid, 'Back 'er tawards tha fier boay, thet waay sha's gotta cum ta-wards ee.'

Cemetery

Thus up tha countray visitur wen down Portleven churchyard fer a geek roun'. Antnee Bolitho waas theer earnun a shillun or two fillun a grave en.

Tha up tha countray fella sid, 'Xcuse me, cud yew tell me wat tha R I P stans fer un oall tha 'edstones?'

'Reared In Porthleven,' Antnee rayplied, standun back ta admire es andy work.

Quickee

Missus Laity 'n' Decky Bray wen un a Band ov Hope charaban trep ta Plymeth. Soon es thay got theere thay wen fer a bit ov crouse en a cafe un tha Bar-be-caan.

Missus Laity ordur'd 'Mayflower salud', wech cordun ta tha menu wud maake ee wish yew set saale bout hower ago.

Decky Bray ask'd tha waitruss fer 'a quickee'.

Tha waitruss slapped Decky en tha chacks. Missus Laity tack-full-lay xplan'd et waas prenounce 'quiche'.

Buz Stop

Tha buz pult up owtside ov tha village pub. Tha buz drivur luked et es watch.

A passenger ax'd, 'Ave I got time few a queck wan en tha pub?'

'Iss,' waas the drivur's rayply.

'Ow dos I knaw yew'r not gwain ta drive ovv wethowt me?' tha passenger ax'd.

'Cos yew'r buyun me a pint es wull!' tha drivur ansur'd.

Identicaal Twins

Harry lukes a lot like Barry, but Barry dudden luke a bit like Harry.

Rugby Playhur Un 'Oldaay

A rugby playhur waas down ere un holdaay fram up tha countray. Ee drove owt inta tha countray ta ave a picnic weth es missus.

Aftur tha picnic thay wen ta git back en tha caar an theer waas a wasp flyun roun en tha caar. Thay rugby playhur waas ta afeard ta git back en tha caar.

Es missus sid, 'Giss un weth ee, tis onlaay a wasp.'

'Iss, I knaw,' tha rubgy playhur rayplied, 'but ets wearun Cornwall Rugby cullurs.'

Postal Charges

Mawthur: 'Furst class stamps es gon up again.'

Faathur: 'I caan membur wen yew cud git a shillun stamp fer a tanner.'

Wan ana Aff

'Wan ana aff ta Falmuff ef yew plais,' Jaw ax'd tha buz cunductur.

'Scuse me,' tha cunductur sid befowour turnun ta Jaw's maaid Susie, 'ow oald ar ee me luver?'

'Fowur en tha 'ouse an thray en tha buz!' Susie ansur'd ta tha best ov er knawledge.

Rhubarb

Decky Bray waas pushun a wheelbarraw ov dung down tha laane.

Missus Laity luked ovur er gaate un ax'd, 'Wheer ee gwain weth thet dung?'

'Gwain ta put et un me rhubarb!' Decky ansur'd.

'I doan't knaw wat tha werld es cummun ta, I oallwaays ave custurd un mine,' Missus Laity grezzled.

Signun On Day

Jack wen down tha Dole Ovvus ta sign un. Tha clerk sid, 'I've gotta summit ere thet mite enteress yew Jack, tes ninetay poun' a week.'

'Es et a tax rebate?' Jack ax'd.

Marvellus Newspaapur

Missus Laity lost er gold waatch; sha cudden find en naw wheere. So sha rung up tha 'Cornishman' newspaapur askun obem ta putt et en tha lost 'n' found secshun.

Un 'Cornishman' daay Missus Laity pick'd up tha paapur ta read weth a cup ov tay. Sha opuned er glasses case an enside waas er gold waatch.

Missus Laity rang tha editur ta thank im fer es elp an ax'd ef ee cud put an ad en fer er lost glasses nixt week. An seeun tha paapur waas so guden gittun qweck raysults, ta bay fair sha wud offur a rayward.

Burgull'd

Jimmy went enta tha kiddleywink wan evenun as usual.

Tha lan-lurd put a pint enfront of em an sid, 'Ave thet wan un me, I eer yew ad a burglar en yewr ouse laast nite.'

'Iss, tha's rite,' Jimmy sid aftur knockun back a drop.

'Ded ee git anytheng?'

'Iss, ee ded.' Jimmy dohwn tha rest ov es pint.

'Wat ded ee git?' Tha lan-lurd was oall ears.

Jimmy geved ovur es emptay glass fer a rayfill. 'I'll saay ee ded. Tha Missus waas en bed, sha thought et waas me cummin ome drunk.'

Ard Workun Miner

Yew caan oallwaays tell a ard workun miner. Wen ee taakes es boots ovv, an turns em up side down, yew caan see tha sweat run owt.

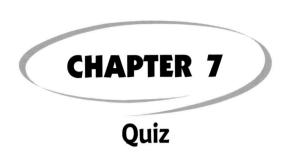

CHAPTER 7

Quiz

Test yourself: here are some typical Cornish expressions – see if you can decipher them. (We've deliberately made them a bit more tricky by running several words together.)

Then rate yourself. Full marks – you've got a twisted mind me ansum, or you've cheated. Half marks – read this book and try again. No marks – move to England. Clues are given in brackets. Answers on page 95.

1. NAWNOWDOEE? (a question)
2. YERANESBLEEDUN (a greeting)
3. THRAYGOALSENE (a game)
4. ETSENTUNDOWN (weather)
5. ETWULLGITEEFRAMATAB (travel)
6. WANFERSARRAW (folklore)
7. VOREAPTHRAW (sport)
8. GONETALIE (corn)
9. WATEEMECALLD (who?)
10. TEWSNWANS (favourites)
11. CHUFFSSTOLETHEERNEST (birds)
12. ESETABOAYORACHIELD? (birth)
13. GUDUNDERSTANDUNS (boots)
14. HEVVAHEVVAHEVVA (fishing)
15. LAVETHAENDGO (boat)
16. EESSUMPUSHIE (ambition)
17. ILLDOETDRECKLY (a promise)
18. GEVETHAFIERAPOKE (teatime)
19. OVAETHAMOON (high spirits)
20. GWAINOMEFAST (the end)

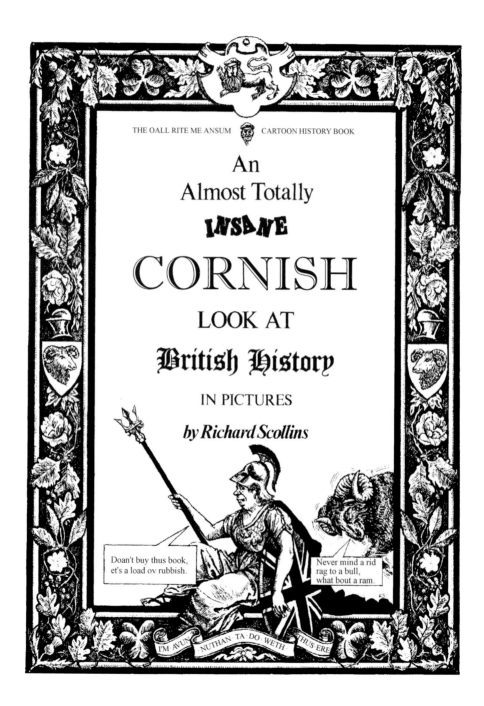

THE OALL RITE ME ANSUM CARTOON HISTORY BOOK

An
Almost Totally

INSANE

CORNISH

LOOK AT

British History

IN PICTURES

by Richard Scollins

Doan't buy thus book, et's a load ov rubbish.

Never mind a rid rag to a bull, what bout a ram.

I'M·AVUN·NUTHAN·TA·DO·WETH·THUS·ERE

Alfred and the Cakes — 878

Lady Godiva — 1057

The Battle of Hastings — 1066

The Death of William Rufus — 1100

King John and Magna Carta — 1215

Edward I Presents His Son as
Prince of Wales — 1284

Bruce and the Spider — 1306

The Battle of Agincourt — 1415

Richard III at Bosworth — 1485

Henry VIII and Anne Boleyn — 1529

Raleigh and the Puddle — 1581

Francis Drake Goes Bowling — 1588

The First Night of 'Hamlet' — 1601

The Gunpowder Plot — 1605

The Execution of Charles I — 1649

**Charles II and Friends Hide From
the Roundheads — 1651**

Isaac Newton Discovers Gravity — 1666

**Bonnie Prince Charlie Arrives
in Scotland — 1745**

Nelson at Trafalgar — 1805

Wellington Inspects His Troops — 1815

The Charge of the Light Brigade — 1854

Stanley Greets Dr. Livingstone — 1871

Queen Victoria 'Not Amused' — 1878

THA END

Quiz Answers

1. Know now, do you?
2. Your hand is bleeding.
3. Three goals and in.
4. It's raining heavily.
5. It will get you from A to B.
6. One for sorrow.
7. Fore hip throw.
8. Gone to lie.
9. What's he called?
10. Twos and ones.
11. Choughs stole their nest.
12. Is it a boy or a girl?
13. Good understandings.
14. Hevva hevva hevva.
15. Leave the end go.
16. He's some pushie.
17. I'll do it soon.
18. Give the fire a poke.
19. Over the moon.
20. Going home fast (dying).

BIBLIOGRAPHY

A ll the following books/periodicals have been used for research purposes; where I have used a direct quotation, the source is acknowledged in the text. All the books are available for callers at The Cornwall Centre, Kresenn Kernow, Alma Place, Redruth, Cornwall TR15 2AT (telephone: 01209 216760). The opening hours are Monday to Friday 10 am to 6 pm; Saturday 10 am to 4 pm.

The Art of Cornish Wrestling – Bryan H. Kendall
Cornish Magazines 1898
Cornish Names – T.F.G. Dexter
Cornish Sayings, Superstitions and Remedies – Kathleen Hawke
Cornish Seines and Seiners – Cyril Noall
Cornwall and its People – A.K. Hamilton Jenkin
A Dictionary of Cornish Dialect Words – W.F. Ivey
General View of the Agriculture of the County of Cornwall – G.B. Worgan
A Glossary of Cornish Dialect Words – Kathleen Hawke
A Glossary of the Cornish Dialect – K.C. Phillipps
A Glossary of Mining Terms – W.G. Orchard
Glossary of Cornish Dialect – F.W.P. Jago
Journals of Old Cornwall
A Londoner's Walk to the Land's End – Walter White
Polkinghorne v Cann – A. Ivan Rabey
Portrait of Cornwall – Claude Berry
Sportsmen of Cornwall – Michael George
The Story of the Cornish Language – P. Berresford Ellis
The Story of Cornwall – A.K. Hamilton Jenkin
Survey of Cornwall – Richard Carew